vabnf   VAL
248.843 CAMPB

Campbell, Colleen Carroll, 1974-
Holy perfectionists
33410015350319   05/22/19

W9-AXH-701

Valparaiso Public Library
103 Jefferson Street
Valparaiso, IN 46383

Praise for

THE HEART OF PERFECTION

"Catholics and Protestants have much to learn from the 'saints' and from this self-revealing book by Colleen Carroll Campbell. Colleen unveils the reality discovered by many who have gone before us that true satisfaction, peace, and joy are not the results of our efforts to live a perfect life, but come as a gift of God's love. To all who are burdened with shame and guilt in their efforts to do life right, the message of this book is liberating."

—Gary D. Chapman, Ph.D., *New York Times*
bestselling author of *The Five Love Languages*

"In *The Heart of Perfection*, Colleen Carroll Campbell explores the real lives of saints with the scrutiny of an investigative journalist and highlights their quest for the perfect love of God. . . . Like so many women (and men) today who are caught in the endless hamster wheel of trying to be perfect, Campbell spent her life striving for her ideal self, and surpassed her own goals. . . . In this deep and thoughtful reflection on herself, the generations of perfectionist women she came from, and with a broad-daylight exposé of the lives of the not-so-perfect saints, Campbell realizes that setting the bar so high is detrimental; trying to be perfect only results in beating yourself up for not being perfect. *The Heart of Perfection* is a must-read for those of us whose pursuit of perfection is just creating the 'perfect' trap."

—Jeannie Gaffigan, writer and executive producer
of *The Jim Gaffigan Show*

"This book is absolutely excellent and meets a very present need of many people. I wish it to be read by everyone! Not always consciously, we are marked by a certain perfectionism, the feeling that to deserve God's love and the love of others we must be perfect beings and follow a faultless journey to God. This perfectionism may seem generous and express the commitment to be good Christians, but it is actually disastrous. . . . From her personal experience, from the example of the saints, from her meditation on Scripture, Colleen shows us with great spiritual truth and psychological sharpness how this perfectionism manifests itself, its consequences, and how to get rid of it to enter into the true freedom of the children of God. One thing that gives me great joy in this book is to see how a woman, wife, and mother, engaged in a very active professional life, living in the complicated context of our society, can reach such an authentic experience of God and deep spiritual wisdom—something that may have been thought to be reserved for some particular vocations, such as religious life. This is an immense encouragement to lay people today who sometimes think that struggling with the problems of everyday family life may be an impediment to progress in the spiritual life. Colleen shows us that it's the opposite, and we should be very grateful to her."

—Fr. Jacques Philippe, author of
Searching for and Maintaining Peace,
Interior Freedom, and *Time for God*

"With lyrical prose and candid storytelling, Colleen Carroll Campbell unpacks the perfectionism that keeps many of us striving to impress God and others, often to exhaustion. Yet instead of offering the quick fix of self-help platitudes, Campbell draws us into the rich and complex lives of the saints. Separated by centuries and culture, the saints nonetheless become like friends in Campbell's telling, revealed to us as wonderfully human yet transformed by grace."

—Katelyn Beaty, author of *A Woman's Place*
and former managing editor of *Christianity Today*

"Perfectionists already know many of the truths that can set us free. . . . But knowing is not enough. We also need such truths to penetrate our hardened hearts and calm our frazzled nerves. This book is here to help. Through engaging personal testimony and the masterful re-telling of lives of relatable saints, it effectively heals wounds that keep us from the joyful freedom of the children of God."

—Fr. Michael Gaitley, MIC, author of
33 Days to Morning Glory and *33 Days to Merciful Love*

"This is a well-written book for any . . . whose lives feel too pressured, who feel that, no matter how hard they try, they can never measure up to what God expects. Colleen Carroll Campbell, with a rich blend of personal experience and the witness of the saints . . . points the way to freedom from a burden that God never wanted us to carry."

—Timothy M. Gallagher, OMV,
author of *The Discernment of Spirits:
An Ignatian Guide to Everyday Living*

"Comforting yet challenging . . . Colleen Carroll Campbell writes with the confidence and spark of an experienced writer as well as with the contagious personal passion of a spiritual seeker."

—BR. Joseph F. Schmidt, FSC, author of *Everything Is
Grace: The Life and Way of Thérèse of Lisieux* and
Walking the Little Way of Thérèse of Lisieux

ALSO BY COLLEEN CARROLL CAMPBELL

My Sisters the Saints: A Spiritual Memoir

The New Faithful:
Why Young Adults Are Embracing Christian Orthodoxy

THE
HEART
OF
PERFECTION

How the Saints Taught Me to
Trade My Dream of Perfect for God's

⁓

COLLEEN CARROLL
CAMPBELL

HOWARD BOOKS
NEW YORK   LONDON   TORONTO   SYDNEY   NEW DELHI

HOWARD BOOKS

An Imprint of Simon & Schuster, Inc.
1230 Avenue of the Americas
New York, NY 10020

Copyright © 2019 by Colleen Carroll Campbell

All rights reserved, including the right to reproduce this book or portions thereof in any form whatsoever. For information, address Howard Books Subsidiary Rights Department, 1230 Avenue of the Americas, New York, NY 10020.

First Howard Books hardcover edition May 2019

HOWARD and colophon are trademarks of Simon & Schuster, Inc.

For information about special discounts for bulk purchases, please contact Simon & Schuster Special Sales at 1-866-506-1949 or business@simonandschuster.com.

The Simon & Schuster Speakers Bureau can bring authors to your live event. For more information, or to book an event, contact the Simon & Schuster Speakers Bureau at 1-866-248-3049 or visit our website at www.simonspeakers.com.

Interior design by Michelle Marchese

Manufactured in the United States of America

10 9 8 7 6 5 4 3 2 1

Library of Congress Cataloging-in-Publication Data is available.

ISBN 978-1-9821-0616-4
ISBN 978-1-9821-0618-8 (ebook)

Excerpt from *Story of a Soul*, translated by John Clarke, O.C.D. Copyright © 1975, 1976, 1996 by Washington Province of Discalced Carmelites, ICS Publications, 2131 Lincoln Road, N.E., Washington, D.C. 20002-1199, U.S.A. www.icspublications.org.

Excerpt from *General Correspondence Volume Two*, translated by John Clarke, O.C.D. Copyright © 1988 by Washington Province of Discalced Carmelites, ICS Publications, 2131 Lincoln Road, N.E., Washington, D.C. 20002-1199, U.S.A. www.icspublications.org.

Excerpt from *The Poetry of St. Thérèse of Lisieux*, translated by Donald Kinney, O.C.D. Copyright © 1995 by Washington Province of Discalced Carmelites, ICS Publications, 2131 Lincoln Road, N.E., Washington, D.C. 20002-1199, U.S.A. www.icspublications.org.

Excerpt from *The Spiritual Exercises of St. Ignatius* by Louis J. Puhl, S.J. (Newman Press, 1951). Reprinted with permission of Loyola Press. To order copies of this book, call 1-800-621-1008 or go to www.loyolapress.com.

For my children:

Clara Colleen,

John Patrick,

Joseph Francis,

and Maryrose Therese,

who, with their father, John,

are the greatest gifts God has ever given me

apart from Himself.

Every good gift and every perfect gift
is from above . . .

(James 1:17)

CONTENTS

1

AN ANCIENT LIE

For the law brought nothing to perfection;
on the other hand, a better hope is introduced,
through which we draw near to God.

(Heb. 7:19)

I never considered myself a perfectionist before I had children. Perfectionism was someone else's problem.

It was the affliction of those pasty-faced library moles that haunted the campus stacks on Saturday nights, still cramming after everyone else had left to grab a beer. It was the curse of the hulking workout kings who passed entire spring days pumping and groaning in the mirror-lined mausoleum of the campus gym. Perfectionism was what made frazzled mothers stay up all night hand-sewing Halloween costumes and what turned fathers into red-faced sideline screamers or workaholics who missed the game altogether.

A perfectionist was that tortured soul who always seems to

land in front of me in the salad bar line, the one who inspects each lettuce leaf as if sifting for gold and complains to the waiter about the radish shaving someone dropped in the fat-free ranch.

That's a perfectionist, I thought. *And that's not me.*

Now it's true that I've been called an overachiever. In elementary school, I considered a B-plus an abject failure, and I was updating my résumé before most kids could spell the word. I used to return my high school boyfriend's love letters to him spell-checked—in red ink. A journalism colleague once predicted that given where I was at twenty-five, my next career move would be a midlife crisis.

I laughed off such comments, but secretly, I relished them. When interviewers asked my greatest weakness, I proudly offered the stock response I knew no one actually deemed a flaw. "Me? Oh, I guess I work too hard. I'm a bit of a *perfectionist.*"

I always thought of myself as too fun-loving and balanced to be a true perfectionist, of course. I was a little hard on myself, maybe. A little hard on others, too. It was a family trait, just like setting—and meeting—high standards. Who would I be without my achievements?

If you had asked me to square that statement with my belief that we should stake our identity on Christ's merits rather than our own, I would have spouted something about God wanting me to live up to my potential. Maybe I would have quoted that line from the parable of the talents that my teachers liked to quote to me. "To whom much has been given," they'd say, in a solemn, grown-up voice that always sounded vaguely threatening, "much will be expected."

I went through times when my self-confidence was shaken and my achievements could not console me. I wrote about some of those in my memoir, *My Sisters the Saints*. As I chronicled there, my journey through infertility and my father's battle with Alzheimer's disease, along with the saints I befriended in the process, helped me understand my dependence on God in a new way.

Still, my perfectionism—and its central role in my lifelong struggle to trust God—remained hidden from me. Until I became a mother.

I still remember that surreal September afternoon when my husband, John, and I brought our twins home from the hospital. As we clicked our little bundles of pink and blue into their new car seats, we laughed at how crazy it was that we were responsible for these two human beings. It seemed like we should need a license or something.

We'd read the books. We'd taken the classes. We'd received the advice—ad nauseam, as new parents do. Really, though, what did we know about parenting? We knew we'd make mistakes. But which ones, and when? Would we know while we were making them? Or only decades later, when our twins dropped by our nursing home, therapists and parole officers and ex-spouses in tow, to detail each way we'd scarred them?

I had joked to friends about the mistakes I'd make as a mother. Inside, though, it was no joke. I was scared.

I knew from my reporter days about the research on brain development and how much those early years—even those first nine months in the womb—matter. I knew from my own childhood how vulnerable children are, how something that looks like no big deal to an adult can be traumatic and searing to a child. I'd sustained some deep wounds as a girl that no one noticed at the time—wounds, I would later realize, that fed my perfectionism. I wanted to spare my children the same.

How could I do that, given all my blind spots and flaws? And how could I do it while performing all those mundane tasks that had always made motherhood a daunting prospect for me, even as I longed for children: the round-the-clock feedings and diaper changes, the all-night vigils with sick children, the endless repetitions of itsy-bitsy spider and pat-a-cake and peek-a-boo? I'd spent the past two decades interacting almost exclusively with adults. My last babysitting gig was in seventh grade. I desperately wanted these babies, but was I ready for them?

I had figured I would just have to do my best—my very best. I'd love them. I'd pray for wisdom. Then I'd put on my journalist hat and do what I always did when I wanted to succeed at something: research every possible angle, interview every reliable source, test my assumptions, evaluate my progress, and compare my results. I'd work, work, work. And I'd succeed—or at least, sleep peacefully knowing I'd done all I could.

As it turned out, sleep was the first thing to go when my babies arrived. Peace of mind—along with peace of body, and peace in my marriage—soon followed.

After twenty-two hours of labor with my daughter and an emergency C-section with my son, I found myself recovering from two deliveries rather than one. I never slept more than an hour at a stretch in the hospital and spent most of my waking moments trying to get someone to wheel me down to the neonatal intensive care unit nursery where my son was spending his first day and a half of life without me. When we finally came home from the hospital, my terror of Sudden Infant Death Syndrome had me bolting upright in fifteen-minute intervals the entire first night to make sure my babies were still breathing. As soon as I'd lie back down, one would need to be nursed or changed. Then the other.

On it went, all night, every night—and daytime, too—for weeks. John was soon back at work and exhausted. I was delirious with fatigue, still bleeding and in pain. The babies were preemies, so they needed to be awakened every two hours to nurse even on nights that they—or I—could have slept longer. They spent a week on BiliBeds for jaundice. We had to log their every wet or dirty diaper and tote the babies—wrapped like mummies for fear of germs—to the pediatrician's office every few days. There were moments of breathtaking joy, but most of the time, John and I were too tired to see straight. We were fighting and overwhelmed and desperate. "It's like a war," I heard one ex-military father later say, when someone asked him about life with newborn twins. "Except in a war, you sometimes get some sleep."

After six weeks, I finally roused myself to go to my women's book club, which I hadn't attended since before the birth. I felt like hell but needed a few hours away from the babies. A glass of Chardonnay and some chocolate wouldn't hurt, either.

As we stood around my girlfriend's kitchen that night, some-one asked how I was enjoying motherhood. I tried to crack a joke, but tears came out instead. I confessed that it had been rough, even rougher than I'd expected, and I felt guilty for not enjoying it more because I had wanted these babies so badly. I felt guilty about something else, too: my twins' early arrival at thirty-six weeks, which made them preemies, and my son's NICU stay, which deprived him of the mother-infant bonding time that I'd always heard was so crucial right after birth.

My son was fine; the doctors said he had a clean bill of health. And thirty-six weeks is actually term for twins. Still, I was sure that the long walk I had taken the day before the birth was the reason I went into labor. And my early labor must have been the reason for my son's prolapsed umbilical cord, which had prompted his NICU stay. And his NICU stay would be the cause of countless unseen problems sure to follow in years to come, all thanks to his stupid, selfish mother and her Sunday stroll. My babies weren't even two months old, and already, I had blown it.

I remember how one of my friends stood watching me from across the kitchen counter, nodding as I talked. I could see something that looked like tears glistening in her eyes. She was a fifty-something mother of five, including a set of twins. Her children had all taken turns in the NICU. Now they were all healthy and grown—all but one, a little baby girl who had died a few days after birth.

"Colleen," my friend said, in a steady, clear voice I'll never forget, "I don't know if there's a place for perfectionism in any other part of life. I don't know about that. But I know this: There's no room for it in motherhood."

Her words hit me like a floodlight. I felt shocked, exposed—and oddly relieved.

Maybe the traumatic birth I had been forcing myself to relive every day of the past six weeks wasn't the calamity I had imagined. Maybe the case I had been prosecuting against myself wasn't as airtight as I had assumed. And maybe the real threat I posed to my children's future had nothing to do with my prenatal exercise or their premature birth.

The real threat might just be that insatiable demand for flawlessness that I had carried like a leaden backpack since childhood. Now I was transferring it to my children. Loaded onto shoulders so small, it was sure to crush them. It was already crushing me.

I knew in that moment that my friend was right. There's no place for perfectionism in motherhood.

I knew something else, too: Perfectionism wasn't just a problem for other people. It was a problem for me.

You don't have to be a congenital perfectionist like me to have a problem with perfectionism. Nor must you demand flawlessness in every part of your life. Perfectionism is simply an addiction to control and a refusal to accept imperfection in some human endeavor. Looking at our culture today, I'd say a whole lot of folks suffer from that.

What other common thread links today's Tiger Moms and Helicopter Coaches, work martyrs who won't take their vacation days and exercise addicts who anguish over missed workouts? What connects our soaring rates of pharmaceutical addictions and eating disorders, our escalating levels of anxiety and depression, our epidemic of credit card debt and the explosive popularity of cosmetic surgery? Many factors contribute to these trends, yes, but a key driver is our demand for perfection.

That demand falls heavy and hard on women. From the time we are girls, we are told that we must have the perfect figure, perfect wardrobe, perfect career, perfect marriage, perfect children, and perfect house. And we must do whatever it takes to achieve that perfection. So we see women starving themselves by the millions, women self-medicating with drugs and alcohol, women trying to prove their worth by giving their bodies to men who don't care about them—men who may not even know their names—then punishing themselves afterward with more starving or cutting or even, sometimes, suicide attempts.

The age-old comparison game that women have always played with each other is now high-tech emotional blood sport. We no longer compare ourselves only to friends and family. Now we must compete against supermodels with computer-enhanced curves and social media pals whose real lives bear little resemblance to the shiny, happy images they post online. In our desperation to keep up, we do violence to our relationships, our consciences, even our own bodies.

Men don't get a pass from the Perfection Stakes. Consider the "social perfectionism" that researchers such as psychologist Rory O'Connor have linked to rising rates of male depression and suicide. It seems that a growing number of men today feel shamed by their inability to live up to our complicated and often conflicting social standards. It's no longer enough for a man to be a good protector and provider, loving to his wife and attentive to his children. Now he must also be a metrosexual in fashion, a testosterone junkie in sports and sex, a tireless tycoon at work, and a sensitive listener and firm-but-positive disciplinarian at home. All without being late for carpool duty or taking offense at a pop culture and legal system that treat dads as dunces and expendable, second-class moms.

Men who fail to make the cut find few places to turn for peer support. The same society that sets such a high bar for men mocks as sexist or sinister nearly any form of male fellowship other than the stereotypical beer-swilling, obscenity-hollering camaraderie of Monday Night Football.

Perhaps this all sounds a bit exaggerated. Not everyone is obsessed with looks or résumés or bank balances. Maybe you laugh in the face of today's helicopter parenting fads and you wouldn't dream of going under the knife or going into debt to impress others.

I'd venture a guess, though, that if you look within your heart and your life, you can find at least one area where your concern for success or control consumes more attention than it should. Maybe it's something trivial, like your never-ending battle to lose those last five pounds or improve your kid's batting average. Maybe it's something painfully serious, like your lifelong quest to win the approval of a critical parent.

Or maybe it's something even trickier to spot, an obsession with being the best that's disguised by piety. In devout Christian circles, most of us know better than to compete openly over money or jobs or clothes. We compete in other ways, though: comparing to see who has the most faithful children, or the most children, or who has given up the most *for* their children. We may compete over who gives the most time or money to the church or whose family behaves the best at church or who is on a first-name basis with the pastor.

Sometimes perfectionism takes even subtler forms. Have you ever thought that all that talk of God's mercy isn't about you? That if you didn't do all the things you're doing now—your daily prayer routine, your service to family and community, your tithing and public witness to the faith—God might love you less? That He might even punish you? Have you ever told someone about God's limitless love and forgiveness and secretly thought, *That doesn't apply to me?* Have you ever said that you're one of the good ones—the people God expects to know better—so there's no excuse when *you* fail?

In other words, you may not be a perfectionist by worldly standards. But are you a *spiritual* perfectionist?

It's a real problem, one of the most pervasive and insidious of the spiritual life. And it's dangerous precisely because so many of us mistake it for a virtue.

Spiritual perfectionism is that same obsession with control and flawlessness transposed into our relationship with God. It's rooted in the lie that we can earn God's love and work our way to heaven.

Most of us know better than to think that out loud. Yet we often live like we believe it. We spend our days striving to improve ourselves, to acquire virtues and purge vices as if willpower rather than grace drives our spiritual progress. We devour books and shows and spiritual fads that promise to help us mold ourselves into the perfect disciples, the perfect spouses or parents or culture-transformers. We track our fellow believers like competitors on God's bell curve, feeling guilty pride when others fall in ways we don't and crippling shame when we fall in the same ways we have since grade school. We brood over our sins—little or big, already confessed or not—and feel shock at our weakness. In our darker moments, we feel discouragement bordering on despair, and a creeping bitterness toward this God who demands so much that we cannot deliver.

Spiritual perfectionism is the least recognized and most toxic form of perfectionism. Its cycle of pride, sin, shame, blame, and despair infects every aspect of our lives, fueling and exacerbating every other form of perfectionism. Spiritual perfectionism distorts our vision, leading us to view others through the same hypercritical lens we think God is using to view us. It turns our spiritual journey into a slog or convinces us to abandon that journey altogether. And it distances us from our one true hope for healing: God's grace.

In a culture that urges us to follow our bliss and boost our self-esteem, spiritual perfectionism may seem like a marginal concern, a problem only for that shrinking share of the population that still worries about sin. Don't let today's feel-good slogans fool you, though. While talk of sin and guilt is rare, our collective mania for self-improvement is at fever pitch. Millions of seekers flit from trend to trend in a frantic quest for peace and enlightenment. We all know something is wrong, something beyond the reach of our mindfulness techniques and self-help manuals. We just can't figure out how to fix it—because we *can't* fix it, not by ourselves.

Christians know this. Or at least we're supposed to know it. Yet faithful, highly committed Christians often fall hardest into the trap of spiritual perfectionism. We drink the same perfectionist Kool-Aid as everyone else but in a double dose. We're not satisfied with meeting only the world's standards of perfection; abs of steel and a kid at Harvard won't cut it. We also must attain perfect charity and glow-in-the-dark holiness. So we do all the right things, pray all the right prayers, read all the right books, and befriend all the right people. And somewhere along the way, we burn out. The faith that once consoled us becomes a source of shame. All because we've forgotten its central truth: that Jesus came to save us because we cannot save ourselves.

What, then, am I advocating? That we throw in the prayer towel and resign ourselves to spiritual mediocrity? That we join today's swelling ranks of spiritual drifters, rejecting doctrines that make demands on us and treating mercy as a pass to do whatever we want? That's how some in our culture—and even the Church—seem to understand God's mercy: as canceling out or contradicting His justice and requiring no repentance or conversion on our part. Following this logic, the solution to our perfectionism is to lower our standards or accept that the universal call to holiness is not universal after all.

That won't wash. No matter how many people smile at our

sins or commit the same ones, something deep within us—the whisper of the Holy Spirit—tells us that God deserves better. That's His justice. The same voice tells us that we can't do better on our own and we don't have to. That's His mercy. Scripture and tradition tell us the two of them—God's justice and God's mercy—always go together. So the cure for perfectionism must respect both. We must trust in God's grace yet also cooperate with that grace. We must reject spiritual perfectionism without lapsing into spiritual laziness.

That's no simple task. It's easier to fall into despair or presumption than to hit the sweet spot between them. And a problem you spend decades denying isn't fixed overnight. That's especially true when the traits you've always depended on for solutions—your self-reliance and willpower, your illusions of control and motivating fear of failure—are, themselves, the problem. For all the havoc perfectionism wreaks, it's tempting to cling to it because you know no other way.

Then one day, the pain of perfectionism grows so unbearable you can't ignore it anymore. That day came for me in the middle of an ordinary week, years after the initial wake-up call in my friend's kitchen. I can still see its climatic moment in my mind's eye, like a video clip captured by someone else.

It's dusk. I'm nine months pregnant, wearing a thin pink maternity top that barely covers my bulging belly. I should be wearing a coat; I misjudged the weather. Now an icy wind howls across the hospital parking lot to reproach me for yet another mistake.

I'm rushing a bleeding toddler to the emergency room. I want to run to its warmth and safety but I can't. The varicose vein that always flares up during my pregnancies is especially inflamed now; it shoots fire up my left thigh with each alternate step. My lower back throbs from the weight of the unborn baby that feels ready to emerge. Now comes a contraction—a huge one, even stronger than the others I've been getting all day—and I double over, gripping my child's hand as I gasp for air. Salty tears mingled with sweat pour into my parched mouth. *I'm going to go into labor right here on this blacktop,* I think. *Good. I deserve that. I deserve everything bad, because it's all my fault.*

It was a freak accident, the kind that could happen to any kid. But it happened on my watch, right before my eyes, and I could have prevented it. I could have slowed down. I could have checked again. I could have decided not to play Supermom, to stop trying to do so much that I wound up too frazzled to protect my child.

I replay the afternoon in my head. Every scene reveals mistakes. Should have skipped that last errand. Should have asked for an extension on that deadline. Should have settled for a good-enough gift, instead of hauling the kids all over town for the perfect one. I should have served dinner late or ordered pizza, not worried about having the house cleaned and the laundry put away and the car unloaded before John came home from work.

Instead, I did it all. Again. And at the end of another frantic day, just as my hunger and fatigue and contractions had escalated to a point I knew was risky, the accident happened. Now here I am, barely able to stand as I clasp the tiny hand of the child whose body must bear the stain of my perfectionism.

I steady myself with my hands on my knees and a hundred thoughts rush over me. I think of another night I spent at this hospital, when I first became a mother and saw my son rushed to the NICU. I feel the same overwhelming fear and guilt. Only this time, it's worse. The hurt is not imaginary or potential. It's as real as the blood that splattered on my shirtsleeves when I tried, with shaking hands, to bandage my child's wound.

My child will be all right; the injury is not crippling or life-threatening. But what if it doesn't heal the right way? What if every time I look into those sweet, trusting eyes, all I see staring back is my own shame and regret? I have punished myself mercilessly for lesser offenses. I'll never forgive myself for this one.

I think of how angry John will be, how angry God must be. I don't deserve their forgiveness. Or my own.

Then, for the first time in my life, I think this:

Someone should give that woman a break.

I'm taken aback. The thought feels foreign, as if it came from someone else.

I swing my head up and resume my breathless charge toward the ER. A strange calm envelops me as I move through the descending darkness. The familiar chant of condemnation resumes in my head—*it's all my fault, it's all my fault*—but it's quieter now, as if coming from a distance. Another sequence erupts, unbidden: *I have to forgive myself. I screwed up, but I'm the only mother this child has. Have to take care of myself so I can take care of these kids—including this unborn baby inside me.*

I wonder, as I take the last few steps toward the light of the hospital entrance: Could it be that the perfectionist voice that got me into this mess is the same one now telling me there's no way out? And that the voice telling me otherwise is the voice of Truth?

I don't have time to decide. We dash into the ER and the rest of the night is a blur.

The events of that day—both the accident and my reaction to it—made perfectionism a front-burner concern for me. I started praying about it, talking about it with confessors and spiritual directors, and paying attention to the way it shaped my days.

I began to notice how the voice of that inner critic that I had heeded for so long was stealing my joy in happy moments and compounding my sorrow with shame in sad ones. For decades, I had assumed that critical voice was my own, a reliable-if-depressing guide to the hard truth about my life and myself. Now I was beginning to wonder: Was that voice really mine? Was it really right? Was it even on my side?

The more I stopped to analyze that voice, rather than blindly obey it, the more I recognized that it was preventing me from being the sort of joyful, affirming, unconditionally loving mother I wanted to be. It was also causing trouble in other parts of my life: blocking growth in my work, sowing discord in my marriage, and distorting my relationship with God.

That last piece was a particular surprise to me. I had always believed that my striving for perfection, and the illusion I created of occasionally achieving it, was simply who I was. It was how God made me. It was who I had to be to merit His love.

If that wasn't true, then what? Was I supposed to remake my personality and spirituality overnight, before I permanently damaged my kids? How would I rid myself of the countless habits of mind and heart I had cultivated based on those beliefs, habits now so deeply ingrained that I nearly despaired of recognizing them, much less breaking them? How could I do that while retaining those parts of myself that I liked—my ability to thrive under pressure, my attraction to big challenges, and my desire to do my best for God? How could I know which parts of me were perfectionist—and thus must go—and which parts were just, well, *me*?

Over the next few years, as I slowly peeled back the layers of deception and confusion shrouding my long-buried perfectionism problem, I realized I wasn't alone in my struggle for answers. Nor was I grappling with something new. Scripture is rife with examples of believers who get themselves into trouble by leaning on their own strength rather than God's. Church history brims with the same. Saint Augustine may have prevailed in his fifth-century doctrinal battle against Pelagius, the heretical monk who taught that Christians could merit salvation without grace. Yet Pelagianism is alive and well among those whom sociologists Christian Smith and Melinda Lundquist Denton dub today's "Moralistic Therapeutic Deists"—people for whom religion amounts to little more than trying to be a good person, with or without God's help.

The heresy lives on because the false promise beneath it is so intoxicating: "You shall be as gods" (Gen. 3:5). The Lord made the prohibition against idolatry His First Commandment for a reason. Idolatry is our original weakness, the same one that ensnared Adam and Eve. Spiritual perfectionism is idolatry covered with a pious veneer, and the false god we worship is none other than ourselves.

We don't think of it that way, of course. We think we're being virtuous, living our faith with rigor and commendable zeal. For years, I believed—as I think many committed Christians do—that "be ye perfect" meant I must be flawless in the things of God or die trying. I thought perfectionism was something to aspire to in the spiritual life. After all, what could be more important than the quest for holiness? If hard work and determination are the keys to success in other parts of life, isn't that also true of the spiritual life?

Scripture and the saints often seem to say as much. Saint Paul tells in First Corinthians to train for the spiritual life as for a race and "run so as to win" (1 Cor. 9:24). Saint Teresa of Ávila's masterwork is *The Way of Perfection*; Saint Alphonsus Liguori's is *The Way of Salvation and of Perfection*. Almost everywhere we turn in religious media and devotionals, we hear exhortations to *strive* for perfection, *acquire* virtue, and *achieve* holiness.

There's nothing inherently wrong with these phrases. They can be helpful, especially in the earlier stages of our walk with Christ, when we're trying to kick obvious sins and grasp spiritual realities that seem amorphous and unfamiliar.

When these phrases cause trouble is when they convince us to substitute our own ideas of perfection for God's. It's a common mistake. It's made by all sorts of sincere Christians yearning to do their best for God—even saints.

We all know the stories of great saints who started out as great sinners: Mary Magdalene, from whom Christ cast seven demons; Paul, who spent his pre-Damascus days hunting Christians; Augustine, who fathered a child with his concubine and begged God to "grant me chastity and continence, but not yet." While there may be twists and turns in their conversion stories, the climax is always the same: the moment of the saint's full-throttle, once-for-all surrender to God's grace.

But what about those saints who didn't surrender in such dramatic fashion, those who struggled for decades just to realize that they needed to surrender because their sins were smaller or subtler or because they thought they should be able to fix themselves? What about those tortured by deep-seated faults who wondered why, after a lifetime of trying, they still couldn't shed them? What about those who struggled with trusting God or mistook their own vision of holiness for His? What about *those* members of the canon of saints—the spiritual perfectionists?

For a long time, I thought there were none.

I knew the saints could help with other problems; I had learned that back in college. During my senior year, while I was battling an aching inner emptiness that my work-hard, play-hard campus lifestyle and bare-minimum practice of the Catholic faith couldn't fill, my father gave me a biography of Teresa of Ávila. My parents had always loved reading books by and about the saints and Dad urged me to see for myself how this medieval religious reformer could speak to my modern problems. I had my doubts—wasn't I a little sophisticated for those ethereal goody-goodies whose books crowded my parents' shelves?—but I had nothing to lose.

A few hours and a couple hundred pages later, I found myself reeling that this nun who had lived five hundred years before me could speak so clearly to the challenges I was facing today. Teresa's brilliance and bravery inspired me, her wisecracks and self-deprecating confessions cheered me, and her passion for Jesus rekindled my own. I realized that the saints did have something to teach me and that the wisdom of a truly exceptional follower of Christ has no expiration date.

Over the next fifteen years, the stories and writings of the saints nurtured my faith and helped me hold on to it through my darkest nights. Their diverse circumstances and struggles convinced me that holiness is possible in any walk of life, with any personality. Most important, this "great cloud of witnesses," as Paul calls them (Heb. 12:1), drew me closer to Jesus and made me long to be holy myself.

Then my perfectionism crisis hit. And though I was used to turning to the saints for help with my problems, I didn't look to them for help with this one. The more I faced my perfectionism head on, in fact, the more I pulled away from the saints I once loved.

Part of it was fatigue. When you give birth to four children in a little over four years, as I did, big chunks of time for prayer and spiritual reading are rare. Motherhood changed my week-day prayer routine from daily Mass and a nightly Eucharistic Holy Hour to fifteen stolen minutes on the couch while the kids napped, if I didn't doze off myself. I made time for longer stretches when I could, but most of my waking hours were spent in sur-vival mode: caring for the kids, caring for the home, squeezing in work and a quick run and a little time to talk and pray with my husband. My concerns were concrete and immediate, unlike the themes of the books piled high on my dusty shelves. I wasn't praying for transformation in Christ. I was praying to make it to bedtime without a meltdown from anyone—myself included.

There was something else, too. The saints were always talk-ing about perfection. Could all those years I'd spent reading their works and striving to imitate them be part of my problem? The saints had helped me so much in other struggles, but maybe they weren't so helpful with this one.

Slowly, as I started to carve out more regular prayer time and adjust to the rhythms of motherhood, my appetite for spiritual reading returned. I still had scant free time, and often fell asleep as soon as I cracked open a book. When I persevered, though, I discovered something: Some of the very saints who once seemed to encourage my perfectionism were themselves recovering perfectionists. And some of the same works I once interpreted as sanctioning my perfectionist tendencies are filled with wisdom about how and why to combat those tendencies.

The saints don't use the term *perfectionism*, of course. They complain of scruples and pride, plead for trust and humility, and speak of their need to surrender to God's plans and stop trying to make their own. They describe the devil harassing them with sadness and guilt. They emphasize the urgency of accepting God's mercy and not envying another's spiritual progress. They also write about perfection. Yet the way they define perfection is nothing like our world defines it. And their road map for reaching it bears little resemblance to the one I'd been using.

I hadn't been looking for any of this before, so I hadn't seen it. Now I saw it in the works of everyone from Francis de Sales, Ignatius of Loyola, and Alphonsus Liguori to Teresa of Ávila, Jane de Chantal, Benedict of Nursia, Thérèse of Lisieux, Francis of Assisi, and even Paul, the dramatic convert who still struggled, post-Damascus, with discouragement. Not all of these saints were perfectionists in the classic mold, but all grappled in their lives or writings with the classic temptations of perfectionism.

Their wisdom is deeply rooted in Scripture, another place where I discovered references to perfectionism that I had missed before. So many Bible stories, psalms, and epistles speak of the difference between God's idea of perfection and our own, of God working through our weakness rather than our strength. In reading these verses, and commentaries on them by saints who had struggled with the same temptations as I did, I felt I had found a buried treasure, one I needed to share.

So I wrote this book. I wanted to unpack these riches for others who might not think to turn to the saints for help with perfectionism or to seek help for perfectionism at all. I wanted to share how I had seen these teachings confirmed by the dramas and dilemmas of my own daily life, a life shaped by the demands of four young children and all the usual obligations of work, family, and community. And I wanted to explore how this wisdom can help Christians in all walks of life, as we seek to navigate a competitive world without succumbing to its compulsions and trade the bondage of perfectionism for freedom in Christ.

Not that I am a fully recovered perfectionist. This journey for me is ongoing; just ask my husband. Or ask my children, who have been my best teachers. One thing I've learned is that slow, incremental progress—the kind we impatient perfectionists hate—can be a blessing. It schools us in humility, keeps us tethered to prayer, and produces visible fruit as we travel toward more complete surrender. Opening our hearts to the Lord's mercy, even if we can do so only inch by inch, allows Him to heal those wounds we've covered over with perfectionism and draw us closer to Himself and all those we love. That itself is a liberation.

Liberation in this life is not the ultimate goal, though. The ultimate goal is still—believe it or not—perfection. *Christian* perfection. And Christian perfection is not just different from perfectionism. It's diametrically opposed. The very perfectionist impulse that makes us winners in the world's eyes is the one we need to overcome to win eternal life with Christ.

Think about it: A perfect life, according to the world, is one that's perfectly managed, perfectly planned, and perfectly controlled. It leaves no room for suffering or weakness. It also leaves no room for joy. Because genuine joy isn't something we can manufacture or plan or control. It comes from giving God the reins, turning our lives over to Jesus, and allowing the Holy Spirit to upend our plans and explode our expectations.

That sort of radical openness to God isn't easy. As a bishop I know likes to say, "Obedience to God always gets us into trouble." It's a good kind of trouble, though: the kind that forces us to lean into God's grace instead of crowding out that grace with our own petty plans and limits and rules.

Letting go of perfectionism frees us to pursue real holiness, not its self-righteous counterfeit. When you're a spiritual perfectionist, there's a strong psychological incentive to deny your faults and mistakes. Who wants to admit that you fell short, once again, of your goal? But when you accept weakness as part of our human condition, and trust that God can work through your weakness to sanctify you and those you love, mistakes are no longer disasters. They are opportunities to learn. Your sins become easier to recognize, admit, and confess, because you no longer have a stake in pretending you didn't commit them.

Even the experience of sin is transformed. You can look your sin square in the face and ask, with genuine curiosity, *What is God trying to teach me through this? How will He use this mess I've made for His glory and my good?* Paul tells us, "All things work together for good for those who love God" (Rom. 8:28). To let go of spiritual perfectionism is to say, *Yes, I believe that's true. Not just for others, but for me.*

When we surrender our mistaken goal of self-perfection, the life of faith gradually becomes a joyful adventure again. And a funny thing happens: In forgiving ourselves for being imperfect, we find it easier to forgive others. Our relationships start to change. Our spouses, children, parents, friends, coworkers, and even enemies begin to feel the ripple effects of the mercy we've allowed to flood back into our lives. It's been said that perfectionists are people who take great pains and pass them on to others. When we kick the perfectionist habit, we stop passing on the pain and start passing on grace instead.

Perfectionists often fear that kicking the habit will mean caving to sin. That's why it's crucial to remember that perfectionism is, itself, sinful. Our culpability for any given act of pride or smugness or discouragement or despair will vary depending on how aware we are of our actions or how free we are to act otherwise. Whether we realize it or not, though, perfectionism is a denial of God's sovereignty. It's a rejection of His grace. That's serious stuff. We should reject it without compromise.

We should also prepare for trials. Unlike the pursuit of perfectionism, a life aimed at attaining Christian perfection probably won't impress the world or even our friends at church. The saints who walked this path before us faced ridicule, misunderstanding, and suffering. Their lives often ended in apparent failure.

Think of Francis of Assisi, shedding his clothes in the dispute with his father and marching off, stark naked, to embrace evangelical poverty—only to later watch the integrity of his religious reform appear to unravel at the hands of his followers as he lay dying. Look at Mother Teresa of Calcutta, striking out alone at age thirty-seven to start a street ministry in India's slums, then spending the next fifty years suffering secret desolation while laboring for a God whose love she could no longer feel. Consider Thérèse, dying at age twenty-four in a French convent where the other nuns fretted that they'd have nothing to write in her obituary because she was so unremarkable, or her recently canonized father, Louis, who spent some of his last years institutionalized for dementia, an experience he hailed as a chance to whittle away his pride. Then there's Paul, who gave up a life of living and thriving by the Mosaic law to become an itinerant preacher of a Gospel that got him whipped, beaten with rods, stoned, shipwrecked, robbed, hunted, betrayed, deprived of food, water, and sleep, left in the cold, and tormented by anxiety—not to mention harassed by that "thorn in my flesh, a messenger of Satan sent to torment me and keep me from becoming proud" (2 Cor. 12:7).

The way of Gospel perfection is the narrow way, and it doesn't always make sense. The world's idea of perfection—as command and control, a rigidly enforced flawlessness—often suits us better. It's certainly a clearer target to aim for. Impossible to hit, maybe, but it has a comfortable concreteness about it. We can understand that standard of perfection. We can complain about it, chafe against it, and fall short of it, but it fits our human way of thinking.

That should be our first clue it's the wrong approach. "For as the heavens are higher than the earth," God tells us in Isaiah, "so are My ways higher than your ways, and My thoughts higher than your thoughts" (Isa. 55:9). As human beings, our thoughts naturally tend toward control. We want to retain control of our lives, even our spiritual lives. As miserable as spiritual perfectionism makes us, we fear that the alternative—to surrender completely to God's surprising will—may be worse.

The saints feared that, too. Many struggled for years to surrender to God, to give Him permission to show His power through their weakness. Once they began to make that surrender, though, they discovered the deep-down, lasting joy that comes only from

God. Even Mother Teresa, tormented by feelings of divine rejection, wrote these words in the thick of her darkness: "Today really I felt a deep joy—that Jesus can't go anymore through the agony—but that He wants to go through it in me.—More than ever I surrender myself to Him.—Yes—more than ever I will be at His disposal."

Surrender—like joy—is at the heart of Gospel perfection. And it's the antithesis of perfectionism.

Not everyone wants us to reach that surrender. The "powers and principalities" that Paul warns about in his Letter to the Ephesians are actively working against our efforts to loosen the chains of perfectionism. Because if we do, we'll draw closer to Jesus and draw other souls closer to Him, too. The devil doesn't want that. He'll do whatever he can to get us back on the hamster wheel of perfectionism.

I don't mean to get all woo-woo on you, talking about Satan. I know it's easy to be misinterpreted when you mention such things, to sound as if you see evil spirits lurking behind every bush. We know that in the battle between good and evil, Christ is the Victor. He doesn't want us to waste time fixating on the loser.

Yet Jesus also warns us against being naïve about the opposition we'll face if we follow Him. "Be wise as serpents and innocent as doves," Jesus said, when commissioning His disciples (Matt. 10:16). That advice goes for us, too. There are eternal consequences riding on the outcome of our battle to break free of perfectionism, discouragement, and despair. We need to know what we're up against and prepare accordingly.

One way to do that is to look at the saints who have left us their exit strategies. Another is to apply those strategies to our modern lives. This book does both.

In the chapters that follow, I draw from Scripture, the lives of the saints, and snapshots from my own life to show the subtle ways that spiritual perfectionism ensnares us and the tactics and truths we need to escape its grip.

I don't offer quick fixes. There aren't any. And pretending otherwise only fuels our perfectionist delusions.

What I offer, instead, are stories. Some are from my own life, a messy work in progress. Others are from the lives of the saints, those flawed-but-fascinating perfectionists who stumbled into the same quicksand as we do and somehow found their way out. The interplay between the two—between our contemporary dilemmas and the dilemmas of saints who lived hundreds or even a thousand years before us—is where I find the richest vein of practical wisdom for overcoming perfectionism. And it is in the stories of the saints, not merely their words, that we see most vividly the lessons they have to teach us.

Each chapter of this book tells the story of a saint—or, in the case of chapter three, a would-be saint whose perfectionism led her into heresy instead—along with stories from my own life and wisdom from Scripture. Taken together, these elements illumine in each chapter a particular aspect of perfectionism we need to resist, a particular tactic of resistance we need to embrace, or, in the case of the last two chapters, a particular challenge that arises when we begin to change our perfectionist ways and discover that other parts of our lives must change, too.

All that resistance and change adds up to a tall order. We can't accomplish any of it without God's grace. With Him, though, "nothing will be impossible" (Luke 1:37).

If anything you've read so far rings true—if you've ever found yourself locked in a cycle of self-sufficiency and self-loathing and wondered how to get out; if you've ever longed to stop competing and comparing and just start living; if you've ever worried that your high standards are choking the life out of your marriage or your children or your own soul—do it now. Take the first step on this road toward true Christian perfection, the only kind worth pursuing. Join me as we journey toward freedom.

"If the Son frees you," Jesus tells us, "you will be free indeed" (John 8:36).

Let's do it. Let's let Him free us.

Let's begin today.

2

THE STRUGGLE FOR GENTLENESS

Put on then, as God's chosen ones, holy and beloved,
heartfelt compassion, kindness, humility, gentleness, and patience,
bearing with one another and forgiving one another.
. . . And over all these put on love,
that is, the bond of perfection.

(Col. 3:12–14)

It was one of those days at the end of one of those weeks—the kind so jam-packed with violin lessons, soccer practices, scout meetings, play dates, and church gatherings that you want to drop dead by Friday night. You can't, of course. Saturday dawns and you're back on the crazy train, dashing all over town to run overdue errands and tote kids to those can't-miss activities that are always more manageable in theory than in reality.

I was in my second year of homeschooling and still locked in the slightly frantic mind-set of a newbie, seizing on every worthy extracurricular opportunity lest my twin first-graders suffer that dread lack of socialization that everyone warns you about. My homeschoolers were socializing, all right. They were up to their ears in it. And I was dog-tired.

Plus, I was late—chronically late, it seemed—but on this particular day, I was late for my cousin's baby shower. My husband and I had done a quick kid swap at home; Saturday was his day with the kids and my day to write, though our full schedule sometimes scuttled that plan. Today was one of those days. Now six-year-old Maryrose and I were back in the car, charging from our home in Alexandria, Virginia, to the home of my aunt and uncle in Leesburg, a full hour away.

I felt tense and frazzled from a week of too much rushing, too little sleep, and too little prayer. John saw it in my eyes as he leaned into the open car window to kiss me good-bye. "You've got four young kids," he said. "It's OK to be a little late."

I pretended to agree. I pretended again a few minutes later, when Maryrose piped up from the backseat to repeat to me the advice I'd given her dozens of times.

"Just do your best, Mommy. All we have to do is our best."

That's not good enough for me, I thought. *Fine for you. Not for me.*

I knew arriving on time to a baby shower was a minor concern. I knew I should relax and enjoy this rare one-on-one time with my oldest daughter, who was thrilled to join me for an outing with no siblings in tow. I knew it was silly to worry how I would be judged for tardiness to an event where I was a bit player at best.

It wasn't unprecedented, though. I always felt nervous when heading to large family gatherings, particularly with my mother's side of the family. My relatives were warm and friendly and full of laughter, but as in many large families, that chorus of laughter could turn against you. My mother had been on the wrong end of family jokes more than her share; she wasn't my grandmother's favorite and that fact wasn't lost on her siblings. So the bar for family approval always seemed extra high for my brother and me.

I tried to clear it as best I could, showing up to my grandparents' house every Thanksgiving and summer vacation with my best clothes, best haircut, best straight-A report card, and plenty of programs and pictures to prove starring roles in school plays and winning streaks in softball and too many friends to count. My brother used to call it our circus act. And no matter how hard I worked on mine, it always seemed to fall flat.

None of the relatives I was planning to see at the shower that day were ones who had teased me. But they were part of a family ecosystem in which shy and sensitive little girls like the one I had been—girls too polite to talk back and too timid to deflect ridicule or assaults on their innocence—fared poorly.

I didn't want to re-enter that ecosystem late and looking silly. So when the standstill traffic of the Washington suburbs finally gave way to the blissfully empty lanes of a sun-kissed toll road, I floored the accelerator and decided to make some time.

It felt good. Really good. Right up to the point I saw the flashing lights in my rearview mirror.

"You were doing eighty-five in a fifty-five," the cop barked a few minutes later, as he peered into my car and spotted a wide-eyed Maryrose in the backseat.

Eighty-five. My fingertips turned to ice as I fumbled for my license. What was I thinking? What the hell was wrong with me? And when did the speed limit drop to fifty-five?

I would later learn that the very spot I had gunned my engine was an infamous speed trap. There was no excuse, though. I had risked my daughter's safety and the penalty could have been much worse than the $270 fine the police officer slapped on me. I could have hurt someone, badly. And I could have faced a mandatory court appearance had the officer not mercifully opted to write me up for a lower speed than the one I was actually driving.

I felt shaky and shamed as I slowly edged back onto the highway, now gripping the steering wheel with the cautious terror of a driver twice my age. When we finally showed up at the shower, I was too rattled to enjoy it. I confessed my speeding ticket to every relative who crossed my path, trying to expel my nervous guilt by repeating my humiliating tale ad nauseam to people who probably hadn't even noticed I was late.

My head was still pounding an hour and a half later when the shower ended and I found myself chatting with my aunt and three cousins about my grandmother. It was an appropriate topic for me that day. Grandma Bea—or Queen Bea, as we affectionately called her—was a perfectionist par excellence, the centripetal force around which our family had orbited until her death eight years earlier at age ninety-six.

Grandma's drive and standards were legendary. A music major and aspiring singer who channeled her talents into domestic life after marrying my grandfather in the 1930s, Grandma didn't just raise twelve children and lead nearly every arts and Catholic organization in Green Bay, Wisconsin. She also rustled up her own whole wheat loaves when the other 1950s mothers were buying Wonder Bread, sent her children to school with mini Crock-Pots full of hot, homemade concoctions because the cafeteria fare wasn't up to par, and took in foster children and wayward teens from all across town, plus whichever bunnies, turtles, dogs, and other strays her children found in need of rescue. All while maintaining a stunning figure and marching her dozen little ducklings into 6 a.m. Mass each weekday wearing a pair of silk pumps, matching hat, and dazzling smile.

Grandma made today's Age of the Supermom look like amateur hour. But her flawless façade took a toll—on her and her family.

For starters, that early Mass was only the first of two the children attended each day, since they also went at their Catholic school. All those forced marches to double-header Latin Masses and elaborate family devotions that Grandma orchestrated with such precision figure prominently in the stories my aunts and uncles tell when bemoaning the faith they abandoned as soon as they left home. Most never returned.

As for those adorably dressed babies and pristine floors and perfectly polished shoes, they required some serious upkeep. That usually fell to my mother, the oldest girl and one of the few who kept the faith. A stellar student and admitted perfectionist herself, Mom remembers hiding in the closet to study after midnight when she was young, because she spent the rest of her waking hours caring for babies and mopping floors and shining shoes so Grandma's life wouldn't look as out of control as it felt.

Not that Grandma was lazy. She worked hard, incredibly hard. Even in her late eighties, I remember her creaking around the house making a hot breakfast for a houseful of guests before dawn and tinkering in her dining room at night to pick up crumbs no one else saw. She walked a mile to Mass every day well into old age, until her frequent falls forced her into a nursing home. She sent meticulously wrapped birthday and Christmas gifts to each of her children and twenty-eight grandchildren each year, pulled over to offer rides to struggling strangers on the street, and never let you leave her house without a fierce squeeze and an armload of the best—and most nutritious—rolls, cheeses, and sugar-free sweets.

There was much to love and admire about Grandma. I did, and still do. But there was also much that puzzled me. Why couldn't I ever help her in the kitchen without feeling like a new recruit at boot camp, constantly under fire for doing things the wrong way? Why did she find it so hard to praise my mother and so easy to find fault with her clothes, her friends, even the way she bit her nails? Why did Grandma seem so desperate for affirmation from everyone she passed in church and in restaurants and in her own home? Did it have something to do with the fact that she buried her mother on her ninth birthday and spent her lonely adolescence in boarding school? Was she working so hard at the externals of motherhood because she wasn't sure she knew how to do the most important part, the part that required her to give and receive love?

And why did Grandma seem burned out on her faith by the end of her life? She still believed, but in those final years, I found it perplexing that this woman who had worked so hard to instill the faith in others now dodged my attempts to talk with her about God or the afterlife or even to hang a crucifix in the center of a nursing-home wall crowded with haphazardly taped family snapshots and postcards. "Hang it over there," she'd snap, "below the pictures, off to the side." Did Grandma feel God had demanded too much of her? Had spiritual perfectionism stolen her joy?

I can only guess. For as much time as I spent with Grandma even into my college years, when I attended school in Milwaukee partly to see more of her, she remained a mystery to me.

The mystery of Grandma—how she did it all, and why—was

very much on my mind as I stood chatting with my relatives after the shower that day. When I took the risk of admitting that I saw perfectionism in both Grandma and me, I was oddly comforted to hear that I wasn't alone in driving myself too hard. And I felt validated to hear that others had noticed our family's critical streak, that tendency to fixate on our own and others' frailties.

A few minutes later, as Maryrose and I were pulling out of the driveway and waving good-bye, I knew God had issued me another wake-up call. Perfectionism runs in families, He seemed to be telling me, and if you don't do the hard work of recovery today, your children will pay the price tomorrow.

There was another message, too, one as concrete as that speeding ticket burning a hole in my purse and my conscience. I realized I wouldn't get far in overcoming my perfectionism until I confronted the habits of harshness and hurry that are among its most destructive symptoms. And that would mean trading the tougher-faster-better approach to life that I had spent my childhood laboring to learn for a gentler approach that would come only slowly and with struggle.

See if this pattern sounds familiar: You push yourself too hard or rush too much and make mistakes as a result. Then you beat yourself up for pushing too hard and rushing too much and making too many mistakes. All of which makes you feel worse, leading to more pushing and more punishing and more mistakes.

Psychologists and management gurus call this a negative feedback loop. It's a cycle in which criticism for past failures contributes to more failures and more criticism, reducing the odds of future success.

For perfectionists, the criticism typically comes from within. That makes the cycle feel inescapable, particularly when you're working not only against longstanding habits and family history but also a Type-A temperament and a distorted idea of what God expects of you.

Saint Jane de Chantal knew the feeling.

A seventeenth-century French wife, mother, widow, and nun, Jane spent years struggling to break free of that cycle. She waged her struggle in the same circumstances that most of us must wage ours today: in the midst of a busy, high-pressure life spent raising children, running a household, managing difficult relatives and coworkers, keeping up with social and charitable obligations, and navigating a culture that told her to focus more on looking good than loving God. Jane also waged it while wrestling with an impatient and exacting personality, on the heels of an aristocratic upbringing and a series of traumatic losses that seemed destined to cement her natural severity and perfectionism.

Yet, for all that, Jane became a saint. And not just any saint: a patron saint of gentleness and a founder, with Saint Francis de Sales, of a religious order dedicated to the very virtues of gentleness and patience that never came naturally to her.

The story of how that happened, along with the advice that Francis gave Jane and Jane later gave others, is the best answer I have found to the perfectionist problems of harshness and hurry.

If you want to understand how unlikely it was that Jane Frances Fremyot de Chantal would become a patron saint of gentleness, you can start by looking at her four-year-old self. Picture a smart, pretty, spunky little girl whose mother died when she was a baby and whose father carves time out of his successful law career to homeschool her. She's wealthy, born in 1572 to French nobles with ties to kings and saints, and she knows it. She also knows her Catholic faith, thanks to her father's regular catechism lessons.

So when she hears that faith criticized by one of her father's Calvinist law colleagues, Jane doesn't hold back. How can you doubt that the Eucharist is really the body and blood of Jesus, she asks the man, when Jesus Himself told us that it was? If you don't believe Him, you're calling Him a liar.

Her father's friend parries back, but Jane gives as good as she gets. The two of them debate until the man grows weary and tells his junior sparring partner to run along, offering a handful of sugar plums to sweeten the deal.

Jane takes the candies, marches to the fireplace, and tosses them in.

"That," she declares, "is what happens to people who don't believe what our Lord says."

And that, in a nutshell, is young Jane.

She wasn't the most ecumenical child—most Christians weren't in those first decades after the Protestant Reformation—but what Jane lacked in subtlety she made up for in sincerity. Impassioned, impetuous, and fiercely strong-willed, Jane did nothing by half measures. That included her service to the poor and sick and her relationship with her husband, a dashing knight and baron for whom Jane nursed a devotion so intense she would later regard it as borderline idolatrous.

Not that her married life was bliss. The Baron de Chantal was often called away to join the French king at court or on military adventures. Jane was left behind to manage the employees and finances of his sprawling-but-neglected country estate and to raise their children, the first two of whom died shortly after birth. When her husband finally retired to spend more time at home, he was shot in a hunting accident. Jane, who was still recovering from the birth of their brand-new baby girl, worked feverishly to save him before fleeing to the woods to beg for her husband's life.

"Lord, take everything I have," she screamed to heaven. "Take my family, my goods, my children. But leave him to me."

God took him anyway. So at age twenty-nine, with four children under age six including a newborn, Jane became a widow.

Over the course of the next few years, Jane's life went from bad to worse. Precarious finances forced her and her children to move in with her cranky and dissolute father-in-law, who lived in a gloomy, ramshackle old castle with a housekeeper who doubled as his mistress and their five illegitimate children. Prone to fits of rage, the elder Baron blatantly favored his new children over his grandchildren and let Jane be tyrannized by his haughty housekeeper-mistress, who saw Jane as a threat to her plans to secure the family fortune.

Jane leaned into her faith for strength. She took a private vow not to remarry and doubled down on her penances and charitable work to counter gnawing doubts about the faith that had begun bubbling up alongside strange new desires to give her life wholly to God.

Jane didn't know what was happening inside her, so she prayed for a spiritual director. Her friends recommended a stern and controlling priest who thought the best way to deal with a hard-driving perfectionist was to drive her harder. He put Jane on a punishing schedule of fasting, sleep deprivation, and convoluted prayer methods that left her barely strong enough to stumble through her long days as a single mother.

Then, just as Jane had reached the end of her strength, she found Francis de Sales.

The pair met in 1604, when Jane was thirty-two and Francis, the bishop of Geneva, was thirty-seven. It took Jane weeks to work up the nerve to talk to Francis; her domineering director had forbidden her to seek spiritual counsel from anyone but him. When Jane finally defied that order while suffering a violent attack of doubts that left her too panicked to care if her director disapproved, Francis did not disappoint. He responded with all the patience and sensitivity her other guide lacked. Francis told Jane that God wasn't offended by her dark thoughts as long as she didn't consent to them.

Peace washed over her for the first time in more than two years. When Jane later asked Francis to serve as her spiritual director, he prayed and slept on it, then agreed.

"I think God has given me to you," Francis wrote, in the first of what would become hundreds of letters to Jane. "I feel more certain of it with each passing hour."

Over the next eighteen years, Francis and Jane forged one of the most fruitful spiritual friendships in Christian history. Exchanging letters every two or three weeks and visiting in person at least once a year, the pair inspired each other to reach new heights of love for God and undertake bold new feats in His service. Their most notable shared undertaking was the founding in 1610 of the Visitation Order, a community of religious sisters dedicated to living the gentle, humble spirituality of Mary as expressed in the Magnificat, the words Mary spoke when visiting her cousin Elizabeth and rejoicing in the Lord who "has looked upon His handmaid's lowliness . . . [and] has done great things for me" (Luke 1:48, 49).

From the founding of the Visitation Order until her death in 1641, Jane taught Mary's gentle, humble way to her growing family of spiritual daughters. First, though, she had to learn that way herself. That's where the advice of Francis proved invaluable, particularly in those first six years when she was still living, working, and mothering in the world.

Francis admired Jane from the start. Shortly after meeting her in her hometown of Dijon, he told a friend, "I have found in Dijon what Solomon scarcely could find in Jerusalem: [the] valiant woman" of Proverbs 31. Francis praised Jane for her "strong heart and powerful will" and was so impressed by her thirst for holiness that he planned to write a book based on her letters.

Yet Francis also saw the downside of Jane's intensity. He watched her discipline her children sternly for small faults, grow frustrated with relatives and employees who fell short of her high standards, and prioritize rule-following and strict adherence to her own devotional schedule over the needs of others. Francis recognized that Jane's hardness and impatience with herself were driving her hardness and impatience with others, and both were linked to the flawlessness she thought God expected of her.

"You're too much of a perfectionist about the purity of your faith," he wrote to Jane the year after they met, "just let the slightest little doubt creep in, and you think it spoils everything."

Francis used to think the same way, back in his college days. After listening to debates over Lutheran and Calvinist views on predestination at the Sorbonne in Paris, Francis had started to worry that he was among the damned, that no matter what he did, he may already be doomed to spend eternity cursing the God he loved. Francis was tormented by the thought, barely able to sleep or eat for six weeks. Finally, he ducked into a church near campus and knelt before a statue of Mary. Francis resolved then and there that no matter where he might end up in the next life, he would spend this one loving God. Then he whispered a Memorare—a favorite Catholic prayer for Mary's intercession—and when he stood up, his fear was gone. It never returned.

That experience, and others as a shepherd of souls, convinced Francis that we grow in holiness more rapidly when we focus on God's love rather than our sins. He saw brooding over faults and tabulating progress in virtue as cleverly disguised forms of self-absorption, dangerous distractions from the grace of Christ that is the only sure fix for our flaws. He took a similarly dim view of harsh penances and elaborate prayer regimens, which he saw as more about doing our own will than God's. As for urgent desires to attain holiness and raise holy children, Francis believed that trying to rush and push spiritual growth—like trying to rush and push children to learn new skills—backfires.

"Be on your guard against haste and worry," he writes, "for nothing hinders us more on our journey toward perfection."

Francis urged Jane to wait patiently on God to change her and those she loved. Correct your children's faults but "do this like the angels," he said, with tender encouragement, respect for their freedom, and none of the harshness or hectoring that only makes children rebel more. Practice self-denial not by starving yourself and losing sleep—Francis told Jane that she needed at least seven or eight hours a night—but with more subtle, targeted penances, such as fasting from a favorite food or answering cheerfully when interrupted. Francis believed that the best sacrifices are not the ones we choose but the ones that choose us:

those frustrations, anxieties, and aches of everyday life that challenge us to respond with patience and love rather than irritation and anger.

In prayer, Francis advised Jane to offer simple prayers from the heart rather than following the long, complex methods her other director had pushed. He encouraged her to receive Holy Communion more frequently and to wait on the Lord for answers rather than darting in a new direction each time inspiration struck. "Do not go chasing eagerly after vain longings," he says, "and I would even go so far as to say, do not be eager in avoiding eagerness. Keep quietly on along your way, for it is a good way."

It was challenging advice for a woman who rode nine miles each way to daily Mass and even branded the name of Jesus on her chest to scare off suitors after her husband's death. Jane was a spiritual sprinter. Trying to do too much too soon was all she knew.

"I am never satisfied, but I do not know why," she complained to Francis.

"Is it not because the very multitude of your desires encumber your soul?" he answered. "I, too, have suffered from that disease."

The antidote, for Francis, was gentleness. A fruit of the Holy Spirit cited by Paul in his Letter to the Galatians, gentleness typically expresses itself in kind words and calm responses to the people and things that upset us. Yet those external expressions are merely means of cultivating the much greater interior gift of gentleness: the peace of a recollected soul that can maintain its equilibrium no matter what disasters, disturbances, and delays come its way.

Our world tends to equate gentleness with cowardice or enabling. But Francis saw gentleness as a sign of spiritual strength.

"Nothing is so strong as gentleness," he says, "and nothing so gentle as real strength."

We see that strength in Jesus, whose supreme courage in embracing death on the cross was matched only by His surpassing tenderness in forgiving the people who put Him there. It's not for nothing that Paul cites self-control alongside gentleness and patience in his list of the fruits of the Holy Spirit. These are gifts of grace, yes, but they come only to those who "have crucified their flesh with its passions and desires" (Gal. 5:24).

For spiritual perfectionists, those passions and desires include our need for speed and our appetite for flawless performance. Crucifying them means admitting our limits, our inability to do everything we want to do as soon as we want and as well as we want. It means consenting to look like less in the eyes of others who mistake our gentleness and patience for indifference, inadequacy, or loss of ambition.

When we face those penalties for pursuing a standard of excellence the world doesn't recognize, we discover the fortitude that gentleness requires. We also discover the challenge implicit in those words Jesus speaks in the Gospel of Matthew: "Take My yoke upon you and learn from Me, for I am gentle and humble of heart, and you will find rest for your souls" (Matt. 11:29). The Lord isn't inviting only natural-born gentle types to learn from Him. He's inviting all of us—hard-driving, quick-tempered, get-it-done-yesterday spiritual perfectionists, too—to trade the yoke of our own expectations and demands and deadlines for His.

It's a tough trade some days, and we can't make it without God's grace. That's true for anyone who would practice genuine biblical gentleness and patience, as opposed to its passive-aggressive or people-pleasing counterfeits. It's particularly true for spiritual perfectionists, who often find the quiet sacrifices required to attain gentleness daunting, even excruciating.

The good news is that our aversion to those sacrifices can make the attainment of these misconstrued and underrated virtues all the sweeter—and even, in the case of someone like Jane, heroic.

"Whoever can preserve gentleness amid sorrows and weakness, and peace amid the hassles and multiplicity of daily affairs," Francis writes, "that person is almost perfect."

Gentleness may be a key biblical virtue, but its cultivation can be a scary proposition in a world that too often tells nice girls and guys to sit down and shut up. Many of us have spent a lifetime learning to talk back to the voices that define Christian meekness as mousiness and patience as infinite pliability. We worry that softening our hard edges could mean losing our edge altogether, surrendering the spunk and drive that make us ourselves and make us free.

Francis got that. He knew that perfectionists like Jane crave and deserve freedom. Yet he also knew that freedom is one of the first things to go when we allow perfectionist harshness and hurry to run—and ruin—our lives.

Jane may have looked like a control freak, but she was the one being controlled: by her expectations, by the demands of others, by the dictates of the angry idol she had substituted for the living God. Francis wanted Jane to practice gentleness and patience so that she could reclaim what he described as "the liberty of the children [of God] who know that they are loved," echoing Paul's Letter to the Romans. This freedom enables us to love God for His own sake and accept trials and disruptions of our plans without losing our peace or fearing God's or another's displeasure. It is a gift of God and an outgrowth of gentleness that in turn fosters more gentleness. As Francis explains,

> *The effects of this freedom are a great calmness of spirit, a great gentle-*
> *ness and forbearance toward all that is not sin or danger of sin; it's this*
> *gentle mood [that is] open to doing acts of all virtue and charity. . . .*
> *The opportunities [to exercise] this freedom are all those things that*
> *happen against our inclinations; for whoever isn't bound to his own*
> *inclinations does not become impatient when things don't go his way.*

Such freedom is a use-it-or-lose-it proposition. If we put it into practice through daily acts of gentleness and patience toward ourselves and others, it grows. If we neglect it by lapsing into harshness and hurry and excessive self-criticism, it begins to slip away. Every day, every moment, presents a new choice. And all those choices—to greet a rude sales clerk with snark or a smile, to discipline a child with loving firmness or fiery condemnation, to skip meals and sleep to meet a deadline or take a breather to care for the body God gave us—help shape us into the people we become by the end of our lives. They determine whether we'll spend our years locked in that negative feedback loop or steadily progressing toward transformation in Christ.

Jane wanted her freedom. And she trusted Francis to help her find it again. So little by little, she put his ideas into action.

Instead of fasting to the point of exhaustion, the once-picky eater practiced "holy indifference" by letting a servant select her food for her, choosing each day to eat one dish that she didn't like, and saving the best morsels for the poor. Jane stopped chasing ever-harsher penances and focused instead on practicing gentleness with her children, her father-in-law, even his housekeeper-mistress. When friends badmouthed her in-laws, Jane shushed them. When tempted to self-pity, Jane pulled out the hymnal she carried everywhere and sang psalms to lift her spirits. Even the neighbors who gossiped that she was exposing her children to risk by caring for lepers and disease-ridden peasants came in for gentler treatment. Instead of snapping back or ignoring them as she once had, Jane patiently explained what she was doing and why.

With each new sacrifice, Jane found new liberty and a greater longing to leave the world and give everything to God. Yet that desire, too, Francis asked her to sacrifice—or at least, put on hold. He knew Jane longed to be a nun. He believed God intended to fulfill that desire in due time, in a religious order they would someday found together. For now, though, Jane's children needed her and Francis encouraged her to find her joy in doing God's will exactly where she was. "Nothing so impedes our progress in perfection as to be sighing after another way of life," Francis told her.

Jane listened, and though everything in her impulsive nature resisted, she waited on God. When the time finally came for her to launch the Visitation religious community, she did so knowing she had followed God's timeline rather than her own. And she took her place as spiritual mother of what would become a multinational religious order, founding nearly ninety convents over the next three decades armed with the little virtues that she first learned in family life.

Just how deeply Jane assimilated those virtues was evident in the way she led her spiritual daughters. Drawing on what she learned from both her children and her friend Francis, Jane guided her nuns with what theologian Wendy Wright describes as a unique blend of "gentle persuasion and encouragement" and "a mother's instinct for nurture and a sensitivity to the varied personalities that came to be in her charge." Jane's letters tirelessly remind the sisters of the need to bear with each other gently, correct each other without harshness, and wait patiently for improvement in themselves and others. This gentle method "is the matchless way to win souls," Jane wrote to one mother superior, "and it is characteristically ours."

Jane still struggled with impatience at times. Her intense drive never faded, and in her early years as a nun, she complained that she was "in too great a hurry to carry out whatever occurs to me . . . due to the desire to get it completed and done with."

Jane persevered, though, and as the years wore on, she gradually grew into a serene and sought-after spiritual guide in her own right. She would enter cities to establish convents and find crowds greeting her with standing ovations. Royals and peasants alike would clamor for her spiritual counsel. Jane found it all baffling. "These people do not know me," she would shrug. "They are mistaken."

Those who did know Jane, and the great cost at which she attained her gentleness and patience, only admired her more. "I regard her as one of the holiest souls I have ever met on this earth," said her friend Saint Vincent de Paul. The Catholic Church agreed, and in 1767, Pope Clement XIII canonized Jane. He praised her many accomplishments but said "greater than anything that appeared to the outside world" was what Jane allowed God to accomplish inside her. Jane gave God permission to take and change what He wished and, the pope said, "her own womanly heart was the first and most complete sacrifice."

There's a story about Jane's transformation that has always intrigued me. It's included in each of the dozen or so biographies of her that

I've read, even the ones that typically sugarcoat her shortcomings. I think that's because it has an important lesson to teach us.

Jane had a longstanding habit of rising at 5 a.m. to pray. In those days, a lady of Jane's standing didn't rise by herself. She needed a maid to light her fire, help her dress, and tidy her room. Alarm clocks weren't invented yet, so the poor servant lay awake half the night, every night, worrying she might oversleep Jane's early summons.

Francis found out and put a stop to it. "Your devotion must be so loving to God and so considerate for your neighbor that no one is inconvenienced by it," he told Jane, who apparently had never considered how her pious routine affected her maid. Jane started letting the woman sleep and took to lighting her own fire, making her own bed, and sweeping her own floor.

It was a small change but others noticed. "Madame's old confessor made her say her prayers three times a day and we were all tired of it," Jane's servants joked, "but the new one makes her pray all day long and no one is put out."

My first reaction on reading that story was to scoff at the whole setup. Jane had a maid to help her dress every morning? Well, no wonder she was so disciplined and pious. If I had personal servants fussing over my children and me, I could find more time to pray, too. And how is it that this holy woman renowned for her selflessness needed a Doctor of the Church to point out that her sacrifice of sleep wasn't much of a sacrifice if it required someone else to sacrifice even more sleep so she could pray in comfort? Seems glaringly obvious to me.

That's the thing about perfectionism, though. It rivets your attention on yourself—what you need to do, what you're doing wrong, how you're progressing or not—and blinds you to everyone and everything else. Jane was so busy meeting this arbitrary spiritual goal she'd set for herself that she didn't realize she was stepping on someone else to do it, that her gotta-do-this-the-right-way-right-now piety was robbing others of what they needed and maybe even souring them on God.

It's easy for me to see this in Jane's life, just as it was easy to see it in Grandma's. What's not so easy is to see it in my own.

Motherhood has helped—especially homeschooling, which has been an education for me as much as for my children. I see every day how my mood affects theirs, how the way I approach a task dictates, to a large degree, how they will approach it, too. If I'm tense and hurried and annoyed, they'll respond with anxiety and petulance and discouragement. If I'm calm and peaceful and gentle, they'll push through and persevere.

"Perseverant, not perfect," I tell one of my daughters, whose hair-trigger frustration with mistakes reminds me a little too much of my own. "We don't have to be perfect. We just have to keep trying."

That's me on a good day. On a bad day, when I haven't had enough sleep and I haven't had a break from the kids all week and my son is flopping out of his desk and can't remember the poetry line I spoon-fed him three times in the last five minutes because he's too busy eavesdropping on the sibling squabble he hears in the next room, I lapse into bad habits.

"We're not going to take a break until you get this right," I snapped one morning last spring, bolting out of my chair and fanning myself with the lesson plan. "It has to be perfect."

"Perfect?" he repeated, his voice suddenly high and plaintive. He looked up at me from his little desk, tears now welling in his eyes. "*Perfect?* I can't be *perfect.*"

Boom, there it was. Now I was actually telling my children to be perfect.

I tried to backpedal, but the words were out there. And in the moment I said them, I meant them. I was tired of patience, tired of incremental progress and good enough and try again tomorrow. I wanted perfect. Now.

Times like those leave me no room to doubt that my harshness and haste affect my children. They also remind me that cultivating gentleness and patience is more than a matter of knowing better or trying harder. I know better than to demand perfection of myself or my children or my life. Yet I do it anyway sometimes. And I can't stop without God's grace.

Grace is always there for the asking. Opening my heart to receive it isn't easy, though, especially on the heels of a dispiriting fall. What I'd rather do in that moment is evade, rationalize, or brood—anything but face my fault squarely, ask for forgiveness, and move on.

Yet that's exactly what I need to do, both for my sake and for the sake of the children who are watching me to learn how they should respond to their own falls and slips. If I refuse to show gentleness to myself and accept God's mercy for my failures, what does that tell them about the reality of that mercy? How does that prepare them for the day that will someday come when their own sin seems huge and God's mercy seems impossibly distant and the devil whispers that it's not worth even trying to recover from their fall? Will they remember my platitudes about perseverance? Or only how they saw me responding to my own sins?

Probably the latter. And what I want them to remember is not a mother who beat herself up every time she fell but one who humbly acknowledged her mistakes, reached out for God's helping hand, and scrambled back to her feet, ready to try again—and again, and again.

"The best practice of the virtue of patience in the spiritual life," Jane says, "is bearing with oneself in failure and feebleness of will." Or as Francis puts it, "Be patient with everyone but especially with yourself."

Being patient with yourself isn't just a good habit. It's a tangible way to break the negative feedback loop in our hearts and our families. If harshness and hurry curtail my freedom and the freedom of my children, gentleness and patience expand it and create a ripple effect of grace that touches everyone I encounter. My daily choices, then—to hurry up or to slow down, to come down hard or to lighten up—have consequences that extend far beyond the bounds of my soul or my home.

Those choices also have the power to sustain or derail my larger fight against perfectionism. I didn't get this way overnight and I won't change overnight. If I don't practice patience after my falls, I'll lose hope and quit before I can heal.

One way to practice that patience is to create new habits and rituals that replace the old ones I'm trying to lose.

I read an article once about a couple working to combat perfectionism in their children. Every night at dinner, all the members of the family take turns talking about their day. They don't brag about successes or gripe about stresses. Instead, each person—mom and dad included—mentions one mistake he made and what he learned from it.

It's a brilliant idea, if you think about it. Why not teach our children early that truth it takes most of us decades to learn, a truth even the saints sometimes forgot: that life's greatest lessons often come through our failures and mistakes? Admitting weakness doesn't make us weak. It makes us humble and real and ready to grow.

Every fall, I dedicate our new homeschool year to Jesus through His mother, Mary. I pick a different Marian title each time, whichever one speaks to the gift that I think we (and especially I) need most.

My first year of homeschooling, I put us under the patronage of Our Lady of Wisdom. It seemed like a no-brainer. I quickly discovered that I needed more than wisdom to homeschool, though. So the second year, I chose Our Lady of Grace.

This year, in honor of Jane, I chose Mater Amabilis. That's Latin for Mother Most Amiable, also known as Mother Most Lovable. Or, as I like to call her, Mother Most Gentle.

On the first day of school, I led a short study on Mater Amabilis with my children, then pulled out a golden-hued icon of Mary tenderly brushing her cheek against the cheek of baby Jesus. It was a gift from my mother a few years ago, and though I had always kept it in my bedroom, I decided to move it downstairs to the wall the kids and I face each morning when reciting our opening prayers, Scripture verses, and songs.

On the mornings I remember to look at that image instead of past it, it reminds me to slow down, to close my eyes for that song of praise, and to relish those tugs on my legs from squirmy little bodies that soon will be too big for me to lift. It reminds me to listen to the words I'm saying as the kids and I repeat that prayer an elderly priest taught me many years ago, when I first starting confessing my stubborn sins of impatience, harshness, and all the rest:

Jesus, meek and humble of heart,
make my heart like Yours.

The icon also reminds me not to rush through the last words we always speak before our lessons begin:

Our Lady of Patience and Grace, pray for us.

Some days it all works. I'm patient. I'm gentle. We enjoy ourselves and breeze through phonics and handwriting and even finish in time to hit the park before lunch.

Other days it's a slog. I burn through my patience in the first fifteen minutes. Everything is an aggravation—the damp weather, my toddler's tantrums, even that repairman who bangs on my door at precisely the moment I finally got my second-graders to stop staring out the window and focus back on their math. I can feel myself oozing edginess and I just can't stop.

I was having one of those mornings last week. And I was feeling pretty good that I had managed to conceal it from my children until my daughter looked up after reciting a flawless rendition of her poem and began to cry.

"You didn't smile at me," she whimpered, rubbing her eyes with the back of her hand. "When I said my poem, you didn't smile."

It's true. I didn't. I didn't realize that I usually smile, in fact, but apparently I do. And she noticed the difference.

So I stroked her little head and gave her a kiss and when she recited her next poem, I smiled. Big.

Now if you'd have told me that story a few years ago, I probably would've said your kid needs to learn how to do her work whether she gets a smile or not. And most days, my daughter could do that. She's a good kid.

On this particular day, though, she needed a smile. She needed some gentle encouragement. When she didn't get that, it hurt.

"Win her by gentleness," Jane wrote once, to a mother superior struggling with her young nuns, "but without giving in to her whims. . . . I realize you are somewhat brusque by nature. Fight against that and try, with God's help, to govern gently and graciously. You will see that all the sisters advance more joyously and faithfully."

It's good advice from a saint who served her time in the trenches of motherhood. I try to remember it when I'm dealing with a child who feels discouraged or needs some firm-yet-gentle direction.

I also try to remember it when thinking of my grandmother and mother and all those relatives and loved ones who shaped me through the years, even if they didn't do everything perfectly. They deserve gentleness and patience and mercy, too, and I can't very well claim it for myself without extending it to them.

I hope my children will do the same for me someday, despite my faults. I hope they will visit me decades from now and find that wherever I'm living, that golden-hued icon of Mary and Jesus is still hanging in the center of my wall. I hope it brings back good memories, memories of feeling loved and accepted even when they made big mistakes.

And I hope that someday, something about the tenderness in Mary's eyes as she cradles her baby will make them think, just for a moment, *That reminds me of Mom.*

3

STALKING JOY

Beloved, if God so loved us, we also must love one another.

No one has ever seen God.

Yet, if we love one another, God remains in us,

and His love is brought to perfection in us.

(1 John 4:11–12)

It's been almost two decades, but I still remember the thumping in my chest when that altar call came.

I was an ambitious young reporter at the time, new to the *St. Louis Post-Dispatch* and working overtime on an investigation of the city's public schools. My social life was crammed into a few hours on weekend nights, which I spent barhopping with other young reporters or mixing with more temperate acquaintances from church.

Neither group was a good fit. The reporters were fun but mystified by my faith. The church friends got my faith but not my sense of humor or passion for work at a newspaper they considered a bastion of godless liberalism. At times it seemed all I had in common with any of them was the fact that we were twenty-something transplants to St. Louis, a city where grade-school cliques endure to the nursing home and newcomers spend years breaking into a social scene that revolves around a single question they can never properly answer: "Where'd you go to high school?"

Dislocated as I sometimes felt in St. Louis, there were bright spots. One was a Catholic leadership group my pastor had nominated me to join, a monthly gathering for young adults from across the archdiocese who were working together to organize a faith festival for our peers. We spent months planning it, and when the big day finally came, our labors seemed worthwhile. The sun shone, the speakers delivered, and the turnout—at least for a shindig planned largely by St. Louis outsiders—exceeded expectations.

I was admiring the nearly full auditorium at the closing Mass when the priest, a lively preacher I'd never heard before, took an unconventional turn in his homily. In the midst of a steadily intensifying sermon on the need for repentance and openness to the Holy Spirit, he lifted his arms, closed his eyes, and began to call us to come forward.

Interesting, I thought, from my perch in a high row near the back of the theater-style seats. *I didn't know you could do an altar call in Mass. Wonder how this will go over.*

There was silence in the crowd, then stirring. A young woman came first. Then a young man, and another. Bodies began popping up. The priest kept praying aloud as more and more young adults approached the makeshift altar to kneel and pray.

Wow. I don't know what's happening here, but praise God. Wow.

My seatmates were less impressed. To my left was a pretty and prim doctoral student, a cerebral Catholic who could quote the Catechism chapter and verse and sniff out liturgical abuse from miles away. She was mad, I could tell. To my right was one of the few native St. Louisans in our group, a nervous-but-kind woman who still lived with her mother and probably had never seen a Mass like this one. That made two of us.

We watched from the back as bodies continued to stream forward, like the slow and steady flow of the Mississippi River. Some raised their hands when they arrived. Some bowed their faces to the ground as if overpowered by an invisible force. Within a few minutes, two dozen young adults were up front, with others still making their way.

Then I felt it. At first I tried to think my way out of it, to readjust my journalist's hat and observe the spectacle rather than join it. It was a powerful tug, though, an almost physical urgency to step forward that I had felt only one other time in my life, when I experienced a reawakening of my faith in college.

That time, the tug had led me back into an empty church to kneel for a prayer that ignited my adult spiritual search. Now I felt God drawing me toward Him again. Only this time He was calling me in front of a crowd.

Please, no. It's too embarrassing. I love You, Lord, but what will my friends think?

I shifted in my seat, trying to distract myself, trying not to feel the heat now enveloping my body. Each time someone else approached the altar, I felt a jolt. I wanted to go.

I can't go up there. I'll just pray in my seat. Jesus, I love You. I'll just love You from here.

The stream of bodies around me began to slow. It was a trickle now, the stragglers. The priest issued one last call.

"Come," he said. "If the Lord is calling you today, come."

Sweat beaded on my brow. My breath quickened.

Don't go up there. You don't have to be a nut about this. Stay in your seat.

I stood up.

It was a split-second decision, just the slightest yes from somewhere deep inside. As soon as I gave it, a momentum stronger than my two legs carried me forward. I reached the altar and dropped to my knees. Tears poured out, cleansing sobs I didn't understand. I felt as if all of my pretenses and posturing were being washed away.

I'm sorry, Jesus. I'm sorry for living halfway for You. I want to live all the way for You. I love You, Jesus. I don't care how crazy I look. I love You.

I felt ravished by love, bathed in a warmth and peace I didn't understand.

Thank You, Jesus. Thank You. I love You. Help me to love You more.

As the moments passed and the tears flowed, I felt an arm slip around me—the arm of that shy friend who had been sitting to my right. She had followed me down the stairs, alarmed by my sudden departure. She looked more nervous than ever as she patted my back.

"Colleen, are you OK? It's OK. It's OK."

"I know," I said, smiling through my tears. "I know."

A few minutes later, we all took our seats again. My friend kept sneaking sideways glances at me the rest of Mass, probably wondering what monstrous sin I'd committed to wind up weeping on the floor before God and the whole world. Normally I would have explained. But as Mass ended and we strode out into the sunlight, I knew I couldn't. I was still trying to make sense of it myself. All I knew was that I felt more joyful than I had since I was a girl, and Jesus felt as close as my own breath.

Then the doctoral student launched her critique.

"He shouldn't have done that," she said, casting a quick up-and-down glance at my beaming, blotchy face. "Mass is no place for an altar call."

She went on from there, dressing down the homily, the prayers, the music. As she detailed each violation of the Mass rubrics, I felt joy leaching out of me. She was probably right. She knew about these sorts of things. I couldn't deny what I had experienced, though: The Holy Spirit had overwhelmed me in the very liturgy she considered an abomination.

After a few more minutes of her diatribe, I summoned the nerve to peel away and walk with another group. I steered clear of her the rest of the day.

A few years later, I read in the newspaper that the priest who had issued that altar call was embroiled in a sexual scandal that forced him to resign his pastorate. Around the same time, I learned more about the Church's wise guidelines for reverent liturgies, including the principle that innovative worship experiences fit best outside the Mass rather than shoehorned into the Eucharistic celebration.

What I did not learn is why God chose that deeply flawed priest and his liturgically incorrect ways to touch my heart. He did, though. I know it. And that touch bore fruit.

From the vantage point of decades, I recognize that altar call as a pivotal moment in my journey of faith. It was a tangible taste of spiritual joy that strengthened me to surrender more fully to

Christ in the years that followed, to shed my self-consciousness about the faith and step into the higher-profile evangelization work that God had planned for me. That experience also taught me that even on my driest day of prayer, I am loved by a God whose longing for me is as ardent as it is infinite.

My friend was right about the timing of the altar call, but she had missed the point. And more often than I care to admit, I do the same.

It happens sometimes in church, when I find myself grading the sermon instead of listening to it, or inwardly groaning at the parents who let their kids sprawl and frolic all over the pew in front of us while I'm trying to teach mine to sit up and sit still. Sometimes it happens when I'm chatting with old friends who work for the Church or in ministry circles and our lighthearted laughter over shared trials devolves into a bitter gripe session about the people and institutions that have disappointed us. It happens even when I'm online, binging on details of some distant scandal over which I have no control, and I find my morbid curiosity and righteous indignation mutating into something darker: contempt, disgust, and despondency over the state of the Church today.

Call it spiritual elitism, factionalism, or a critical spirit—whatever it is, this penchant for fixating on the failings of the Church and its members or of those who don't take religion as seriously as I do is ugly by any name. It's a shameful tendency I don't want to confess even to myself, which makes it that much tougher to uproot.

"Smugness is the Great Catholic Sin," novelist Flannery O'Connor once wrote. "I find it in myself and don't dislike it any less."

It's not an exclusively Catholic problem. Highly committed Christians of any stripe are prone to smugness. We believe we've found the key to eternal life—or the fullness of the faith, as Catholics say—and we forget that's a reason for gratitude, not gloating.

Gloating is more fun, of course. Especially when you spend your days deflecting nosy questions and snide comments from people who can't understand why you have so many children or why you raise them the way you do or why you don't spend your time and money the way everyone else does. It can be tempting to allow your fatigue and resentment to scab over into a self-protective posture of superiority and scorn toward those who don't see things your way.

It's that age-old temptation to spiritual pride, and in perfectionists swimming against the cultural current, it often takes the shape of religious partisanship. As C. S. Lewis explains in *The Screwtape Letters*, the devil rarely tempts us to take pride in being a Christian. Instead, he tempts us to take pride in being the *right* sort of Christian: the faithful kind, the intellectual kind, the orthodox or traditional or progressive or compassionate kind. Once we do that, we begin to develop what Lewis calls "a hothouse mutual admiration" for fellow members of our elite set and "a great deal of pride and hatred" toward everyone else "which is entertained without shame because the 'Cause' is its sponsor and it is thought to be impersonal." Even a holy cause can be turned to evil ends, Lewis writes, once Christians "acquire the uneasy intensity and the defensive self-righteousness of a secret society or clique."

I don't read those words as a knock on intentional Christian community. Fellowship is vital for any believer, all the more so for parents seeking to raise faithful children in today's secular culture.

Admitting you need the companionship of other Christians striving for holiness isn't elitism; it's a mark of humility and spiritual maturity.

The trick is finding a support network without shunning those outside it, living our faith intentionally without becoming condescending and cranky toward those who don't. That's no mean feat in times of complacency, corruption, and confusion in the Church—times like those we're living in today.

The good news is that we've been here before. Other eras have found the Church reeling from both internal divisions and external assaults. Then, as now, the lure of factions and religious pessimism was strong. To understand how and why we must resist that lure, it helps to look at someone who didn't: Angélique Arnauld, a friend of Francis de Sales and Jane de Chantal whose unsmiling spiritual elitism led her into the heart of one of history's darkest heresies.

Crack open an old book about Angélique—a dusty one from the library's back corner, preferably published before 1940—and you'll find this seventeenth-century French abbess depicted as a cross between Caiaphas and Cruella de Vil. She's scheming, stone-hearted, and defiant, the conniving leader of a group of renegade nuns whom the Archbishop of Paris famously labeled "as pure as angels and as proud as devils."

Dig more deeply into her story, though, and you'll discover a sincere Christian who spent decades striving to reform herself and her church. Angélique never intended to foment heresy. She simply wanted to worship God her way, with her kind of Christians, without interference from her theological and moral lessers.

She was an elitist, in other words. And that elitism proved her undoing.

Its seeds were sewn early, in the influential French family to which she was born in 1591. Angélique was only seven when her grandfather cut a deal with France's King Henri IV to have her named the abbess of Port-Royal, a Cistercian convent near Paris. The Arnaulds lied about her age on the documents they sent to Rome to gain official church approval.

Angélique was then shipped off to Maubuisson Abbey to learn her catechism from its notoriously promiscuous mother superior, who lived there with some dozen children from different fathers and encouraged her nuns to take as many lovers as she did. By the time Angélique was installed as abbess of Port-Royal at age eleven, on the same day she received her First Holy Communion, she was so clueless about the Catholic faith that she had to borrow the abbey cobbler's prayer book to find out that the sacrament she was receiving was the body and blood of Jesus. No one else had bothered to tell her.

Angélique spent the next five years reading worldly novels, drifting in and out of depression-induced illnesses, and dreaming of running off to get married like her Protestant aunts while her mother and an older nun ran the convent for her. Port-Royal was a boisterous, profligate place: the scene of costume parties and lavishly decorated apartments occupied by a dozen nuns who couldn't tell you what a sacrament was and overseen by a priest too busy hunting to learn the Lord's Prayer.

When Angélique was sixteen, a Capuchin friar came to Port-Royal speaking of a humble King who left His throne to be born poor, all for love of her. His words lit a spark in Angélique's soul and convinced her to dedicate her life to Christ. She plunged into prayer and penance, tortured by guilt over the religious office she had gained through fraud. When she told another visiting Capuchin that she planned to renounce her abbess position, he convinced her to reform her convent instead.

So Angélique did. And no one—not her family, her fellow nuns, or the prioress accustomed to running things in her place—much appreciated it. Angélique persevered, though, leading her nuns by example to recover their monastic vows of poverty, chastity, and obedience. The sisters gradually agreed to give up their private possessions and re-establish the enclosure that separated them from the outside world. They even backed Angélique as she defied her powerful relatives, who paid the convent's bills, by barring the door when her enraged parents and some of her nineteen siblings stormed Port-Royal shortly after her eighteenth birthday. The Angelican reform, as Angélique's changes to French religious life would become known, had begun.

Over the next decade, Angélique transformed Port-Royal into a stronghold of theological and moral rigor. Her nuns didn't just live simply. They rose at 2 a.m. to pray, ate no meat, bunked in dormitories, wore coarse garments to irritate their skin, spoke only once daily during a recreation period, and divided the rest of their hours between hard labor and highly choreographed prayer. It was a grueling life. And in a culture that equated austerity with holiness, it made them celebrities, the sort of sisters that wealthy Parisians wanted educating their children and leading their retreats.

It was only a matter of time, then, that the famous abbess of Port-Royal would cross paths with the even-more-famous bishop of Geneva. Meeting Francis de Sales was a dream come true for twenty-seven-year-old Angélique, who had long admired him and desperately wanted a spiritual director. Francis, then fifty-one, became a regular preacher at Angélique's convents and added her to his growing roster of regular correspondents. He admired his new friend's reforms but wasted no time in calling out her faults— starting with the stony severity for which Angélique was famous.

"Do not burden yourself too much with vigils and austerities," Francis told Angélique. ". . . Enter the Port-Royal [royal door] of the religious life by the royal road of the love of God and of your neighbor, by humility and gentleness."

Love of God came easy to Angélique. Love of neighbor, not so much. An inspiring but inflexible leader, Angélique harshly judged anyone she saw breaking the rules or scandalizing the faithful. She longed to do great things for God and didn't suffer fools or lukewarm souls slowing her down.

Francis sympathized. As bishop of Calvinist-controlled Geneva—a city so hostile to Catholics that he couldn't even live within its borders—Francis had met more than his share of tepid or lapsed Catholics and their Protestant critics. Yet his commitment to speaking the truth in love impressed even his Protestant rivals, brought droves back into the Catholic fold, and turned his once-anemic diocese into a hotbed of renewal. Charity and cheerful persistence were the keys to his success, and few things rankled Francis more than watching devout-but-dour believers give the faith a bad name.

When Francis heard about a showdown at Maubuisson in which Angélique resorted to sarcasm to score points, he told her he wished she had not "mocked and jeered at those people but . . . enlightened them by the compassion which they deserve." When Angélique complained that Jane had called her "daughter"—a term she found patronizing—Francis praised her candor but gently chided the pride behind what he termed her "nonsense" grievance. As for those corrupt priests and monks who infuriated Angélique, Francis urged her to direct her legitimate frustration into prayers for reform, which bear more fruit than mere griping or gossip. Practice virtue and self-sacrifice "gaily and joyously," he said, remembering that our sanctification, like church reform, is a slow process and—as he reminded her another time—"the perfection at which we aim does not come, dear daughter, for many years."

Angélique revered Francis—she secretly ate his leftover food and preserved items he touched as relics of a living saint—but she didn't take his advice. Time and again in their correspondence, Francis repeats the same suggestions in answer to what appear to be the same questions from Angélique. His letters are gracious, but as Wendy Wright notes, they contain "subtle indications that this friend was not understanding him as well as most."

Perhaps Angélique didn't want to understand Francis. He was asking her to surrender nearly everything that defined her: her austerity; her rash, razor-sharp judgments; the satisfaction she took in upholding church teachings and battling those who didn't. If she wasn't Angélique the iron-fisted reformer, who would she be? If she started letting little things slide and building bridges with her critics, how would she preserve the purity of her reform—and her own reputation?

Francis seemed to know he wasn't getting through, and that probably explains why he never warmed to Angélique's idea of leaving Port-Royal to join the new Visitation order that he and Jane had started. Angélique pushed the plan repeatedly with him and even recruited Jane to intercede on her behalf. Yet Francis remained reluctant to welcome this stern spiritual elitist into an order inspired by the Magnificat, in which Mary "rejoices in God my Savior" as she cheerfully admits her lowliness (Luke 1:46–55).

Had Francis spent more years guiding her, maybe Angélique would have softened her hard edges and found a home in Visitation. But in December 1622, less than four years after they met, Francis died of a stroke. Angélique spent the next decade bouncing between spiritual directors until she finally settled on someone she trusted as much as Francis: Jean du Vergier de Hauranne, better known as the Abbot of Saint-Cyran.

Like Francis, Saint-Cyran was a brilliant and pious priest. But he was more domineering than Francis, harsher in his judgments, and less docile to church authorities when they questioned the ideas he had inherited from his friend, Dutch bishop and theologian Cornelius Jansen. Those ideas included an overly narrow view of who could be saved, an excessive emphasis on human sinfulness, and a virtual denial of our freedom to cooperate with or resist God's grace.

Jansen had died before he could promote his theories, but Saint-Cyran eagerly took up the mantle in his place, adding his own rigid moralism to Jansen's already grim theology. The result was a peculiar mix of moral perfectionism, theological fatalism, and resistance to church authority that would become known as the Jansenist heresy. This dissident movement pulled scores into its dreary undertow, starting with Angélique.

Angélique had always been prone to extremes. And her family had always hated Jesuits. So when Saint-Cyran arrived around 1635 preaching Jansenism and dismissing its Jesuit detractors as too lenient on sinners, the forty-four-year-old abbess was all ears.

That this supposedly grace-based theology came with a heavy dose of moral severity was even better. No longer did Angélique have a spiritual director balking at her extreme penances and spiritual grandiosity. Now she had one shoving her in the direction she already wanted to go. Saint-Cyran armed Angélique with a divine mandate for the disgust she always had felt toward the lackluster Christians who scandalized her as a child and blocked her reforms as an adult.

Angélique soon made Saint-Cyran the chaplain of Port-Royal, a plum position that allowed him to school her nuns, her family, and her many lay followers in Jansenist doctrine. Among his key teachings were an insistence on perfect contrition—the idea that the sacrament of Confession only counts if you regret your sins purely for love of God and not because you fear His punishment—and discouragement of frequent Communion, which Saint-Cyran considered presumptuous for anyone who didn't meet the sky-high standard of perfect contrition and complete detachment from sin.

Neither was orthodox Catholic teaching. Perfect contrition beats imperfect, but the Church only requires that a penitent confess his sins with genuine remorse and resolve to change in order to receive the grace of the sacrament. As for the Eucharist, the Church has never considered flawlessness a prerequisite for receiving Communion, only the absence of mortal, or serious, sin. Catholics are encouraged to confess venial, or lesser, sins but as the *Catechism of the Catholic Church* explains, the Eucharist "wipes away venial sins" while it also "strengthens our charity" and "preserves us from future mortal sins."

Given the link between the Eucharist and charity, it's not surprising that the more Angélique and her nuns adopted Saint-

Cyran's stingy sacramental approach—by adoring Jesus in the Eucharist but not receiving Him—the more they closed ranks against outsiders. The nuns still read the writings of Francis de Sales and Teresa of Ávila that Angélique had admired in her youth, but as philosopher John Conley notes in *Adoration and Annihilation*, his history of Port-Royal, they did so through a peculiar Jansenist lens that stripped away the saints' "aesthetic exuberance and their prudential concern for human weakness." There was no room for exuberance or even evangelization at Port-Royal. The nuns were too busy grimly securing their own salvation to risk contamination from a wider world where they saw sin lurking everywhere, including in pleasures and virtues that appeared to be good.

Port-Royal soon grew into the command center of Jansenism, attracting intellectuals who wanted to breathe the same purified air as Angélique and her nuns. Among them was Angélique's youngest brother, Antoine Arnauld, who wrote a book in 1643 arguing that since the Eucharist we consume on earth is the same food eaten in heaven, we should receive it only if we are as perfect as saints.

The book became a bestseller, and when its thesis filtered down to folks in the pews, the effects were devastating. First in France and soon in churches scattered across Europe and beyond, penitents could be found confessing the same instances of sin over and over without ever receiving absolution because Jansenist priests judged their contrition imperfect. As Jesuit theologian John Hardon describes it, "Jansenist priests were known never to say Mass; others considered it a matter of principle to reduce reception of the sacraments to a minimum, so that Catholics were found who had not made their First Communion by the age of 30." Some Catholics influenced by Jansenism defied the Church's rule to receive the Eucharist at least once a year and even refused the Eucharist on their deathbeds, so terrified were they of receiving unworthily.

That terror led some Catholics straight out of the Church. If God's demands are impossible to meet and you don't have the freedom to try to meet them anyway—if an arbitrary deity may or may not toss you the lifeline of grace you need to make good choices—then why not just hang it up and have a good time? Many upper-class French Catholics did exactly that, and historians cite backlash against Jansenism as contributor to the strident secularism and anti-clericalism of the French Revolution.

Jansenism had its critics, of course. Four popes condemned Jansen's teachings over a period of nearly a century, three of them during Angélique's lifetime. Despite those pronouncements and the relatively small core of intellectuals informed enough to defend Jansen's writings, the movement exercised outsized influence in the Church for nearly two centuries.

One reason was snob appeal: Upper-class Catholics liked belonging to a faction too cerebral for the masses and so exclusive it had its own crucifix. (The Jansenist crucifix shows Jesus stretching His arms vertically, in a slim V rather than a T, to stress that He died only for the elect.) Devout Catholics of lower classes didn't get the details but admired the strict morals of Jansenist leaders and their knack for cutting Enlightenment-era skeptics down to size by stressing God's transcendence.

Angélique struck those notes in her writings, which were often rebuttals to official church pronouncements against Jansen's work. Like many Jansenists, she professed obedience to church authorities even as she fired off copious letters to argue

that those authorities were too dense, deceived, or sinful to recognize Jansen's genius. Under her leadership, Port-Royal became
a citadel of Jansenist defiance—or, as French king Louis XIV put
it, "a nest of heretics."

That nest began to collapse in 1661, when Angélique was
sixty-nine and near death. The king, emboldened by Angélique's
refusal to assent to the Church's latest judgment against Jansen,
exiled Port-Royal's priests and closed its school and training
house for new nuns. Angélique spent her final months battling
physical pain, fearing for the future of her religious community,
and continuing her feisty defense of the Jansenist cause that had
consumed her for nearly thirty years. She penned one final letter from her deathbed soliciting sympathy from France's queen
mother, a descendent of Spain's King Philip II, comparing herself
to persecuted Spaniard Teresa of Ávila—minus Teresa's emphasis
on cheerful obedience, of course. Angélique then heaved her last,
warning her nuns as she braced for God's judgment that, "It is
necessary to prepare for this terrible hour."

Just how terrible that hour was for Angélique we can't know
this side of eternity. What we do know is this: Despite her remarkable achievements—the reform of several convents, an impres-
sive body of intelligent if flawed writings, and the founding of two
branches of the Port-Royal community that comprised some two
hundred nuns at the time of her death—Angélique died at war
with the Church she loved. The religious community she spent
her life working to build died only decades after she did, when
Port-Royal's dwindling ranks of rebellious nuns were evacuated
in 1709 and their convent razed to the ground shortly afterward.
As for the Jansenist movement, it heaved its last public gasp a
few decades later with the rise and fall of the convulsionnaires,

a group that took Jansenism's killjoy ethos to sadomasochistic extremes by conducting graveside orgies in which they tortured each other with beatings, cutting, and crucifixions.

It was an ugly end to a movement originally intended to purify the Church. Even uglier was how Jansenism's pessimistic ethos seeped into Catholic seminaries, convents, parishes, and schools long after the movement's official demise. For generations after Angélique died, Catholics who never knew her story would lose their faith, or nearly so, trying to appease the grim perfectionist idol she helped bring to birth.

I find Angélique's story haunting. Not only her fall into heresy, but what preceded it. Angélique wasn't the villainous "Mistress of Jansenism" those old books describe, a soul hardwired for chronic negativity and contempt. She was a perfectionist with a snooty streak, yes, but she was also a woman who once felt the ravishing love of God and did her best to return it, at least for a time.

She was a woman, in other words, a lot like me. And that means I can't dismiss Angélique. I have to learn from her—or risk becoming her.

There's a line of Angélique's that has stuck with me ever since I first read it. She's describing how profoundly the sermon from that traveling Franciscan preacher touched her heart when she was sixteen. "From that moment on," she writes, "my joy at being a religious was far greater than any of the unhappiness I had felt before."

It's a line I could have written on the heels of my own reawakening of the faith in college or after that altar call in my twenties. It's a line that any of us who know Jesus in a personal way could write.

Its familiarity is what makes it scary. Angélique knew Jesus. She tasted the joy of the Lord. Then somewhere along the way, she lost that joy.

That means I could lose it, too, if I'm not careful.

There are days when it feels like I already have, days when judgment and criticism take the place of praise and gratitude, when one complaint snowballs into another until all I can see is what's wrong with the world and the Church and my life. I keep piling rocks on my fortress of judgment until no one is good enough to get in, including me. And I find that I've surrendered my joy—willingly, without even a fight.

Angélique's story, and especially the division and error she spread once pride in her own rightness replaced joy in the Lord, makes me wonder if I've been thinking about joy all wrong.

For most of my life, I thought joy was a fringe benefit of the spiritual life, a nice bonus if it comes your way and you're so inclined. The more I reflect on Angélique's story and its parallels to my own, though, the more I think the prophet Nehemiah was onto something when he said, "the joy of the Lord is your strength" (Neh. 8:10). Joy is not merely our reward or trademark as followers of Christ. It's our strength. And that means we are spiritually weak—vulnerable to sin, error, and attack—when we forfeit it.

When Angélique lost her joy, all she could see was what was wrong with the Church, its members and leaders, and any of its teachings that didn't fit her narrow vision of God. Her faith hardened into ideology. There was no room for the Holy Spirit, no room for God to teach her something new through someone unexpected. There were only good guys and bad guys, those who were on her side and those who weren't.

It's a familiar pattern, and it happens in our day as it did in Angélique's. The fired-up convert (or revert) slowly morphs into the cranky Christian, chronically scandalized by the gap between the Mystical Body of Christ described in Scripture and the anemic, sin-plagued parish down the block. "It seems to be a fact that you have to suffer as much from the Church as for it," Flannery O'Connor said, "but if you believe in the divinity of Christ, you have to cherish the world at the same time that you struggle to endure it."

Living with that paradox—that we need the Church, yet suffer from the sins of its members; that we need to share the Gospel, even though the world will reward our efforts with ridicule and persecution—is hard. It's easier to lapse into division and despair than to keep our hearts open to the joy of the Holy Spirit and those He wants us to reach with His love.

Part of what makes divisiveness so tempting is that divisions are sometimes necessary. Jesus tells us to beware "false prophets" (Matt. 24:11) and the Book of Psalms opens with a warning to flee the "company of scoffers" (Ps. 1:1). Cultivating the joy of the Lord doesn't mean strapping on our Stepford-wife smiles and winking at sin or going with the flow in a culture that redefines evil as good and calls anyone who objects a hater. We find our joy by doing God's will and standing up for the truth, no matter the cost.

But what if part of God's will—a bigger part than most of us perfectionists realize—is that we cultivate joy? And if refusing to do so is a form of disobedience, a rejection of the Holy Spirit?

It's a provocative idea, but it has ample support in Scripture. We are told to "rejoice in the Lord" even in barren times (Hab. 3:18), to offer "shouts of joy" to the Lord (Ps. 5:12, Ps. 27:6, Ps. 32:11, Ps. 47:2, Ps. 98:4), to "rejoice and be glad" in His gifts (Ps. 118:24), and to make His statutes "the joy of my heart" (Ps. 119:111). Biblical heroes often are known, like the saints, for their joy: The second book of Samuel shows King David "dancing before the Lord with abandon" and "with shouts of joy" as his wife Michal watches in disgust. When she scolds him for playing the fool, David answers, "not only will I make merry before the Lord, but I will demean myself even more." The story ends with Michal, not David, suffering God's disfavor (2 Sam. 6:14–23).

In the New Testament, Jesus describes joy as a spiritual gift we must actively seek: "ask and you will receive, so that your joy may be complete" (John 16:24). Paul says joy—not perfectionist rule-following—is at the heart of our life in Christ: "For the kingdom of God is not a matter of food and drink, but of righteousness, peace, and joy in the holy Spirit" (Rom. 14:17). "Rejoice in the Lord always," Paul urges the Philippians. "I shall say it again: rejoice!" (Phil. 4:4). Lest we mistake that command for a suggestion, Paul repeats it to the Thessalonians: "Rejoice always. Pray without ceasing. In all circumstances give thanks, for this is the will of God for you in Christ Jesus" (1 Thes. 5:16–18).

Joy, as C. S. Lewis said, "is the serious business of heaven." That means it's our business, too—not just to hope for joy or wait for joy or ask for joy. We need to pursue and protect joy, to recognize it as a source of supernatural strength without which we can't hope to love others or God. "Picture me with my ground teeth stalking joy," Flannery once told a friend, "—fully armed too as it's a dangerous quest."

We can't create joy ourselves, of course. It's a gift of God, one that Paul lists second only to love in his rundown of the fruits of the Holy Spirit. While the "works of the flesh" include "hatreds, rivalry, jealousy, outbursts of fury . . . dissensions [and] factions,"

Paul says, fruits of the Spirit such as joy help us to "not be conceited, provoking one another" (Gal. 5:20–26). Jesus underscores this link between joy and charity in the Gospel of John, where He says that we draw near God and preserve our joy by loving others: "If you keep My commandments, you will remain in My love. I have told you this so that My joy may be in you and your joy may be complete. This is My commandment: love one another as I love you" (John 15:9–12).

So what does it look like to cultivate joy in daily life through love of God and neighbor? What does it mean, exactly, to be "stalking joy"?

For Flannery, that self-described smugness sufferer, it meant asking God each morning for joy, remaining faithful to prayer and the sacraments, and struggling "to accept . . . with joy" the frustrations of her life as a Catholic writer battling isolation and a debilitating disease in a secular culture where neither Christians nor secularists understood her work. Stalking joy also meant choosing not to take easy offense at fellow believers. "It is a sign of maturity not to be scandalized," she said, "and to try to find explanations in charity."

For me, stalking joy also entails limiting my exposure to negative people and conversations, asking God for the grace to curb my runaway complaining before it starts, and minimizing my screen time, particularly time spent following the news, social media, and perpetually aggrieved pundits, however much I may agree with them. My conscious pursuit of spiritual joy has meant little changes—like listening to praise music instead of secular rock on my morning runs, and big ones—like shifting the focus of my work from lamenting the woes of the City of Man to exploring and proclaiming the riches of the City of God. And it has meant taking Paul's advice in the Letter to the Philippians, where he follows his command to rejoice with a suggestion of what to rejoice about: "Finally, brothers, whatever is true, whatever is honorable, whatever is just, whatever is pure, whatever is lovely, whatever is gracious, if there is any excellence and if there is anything worthy of praise, think about these things" (Phil. 4:8).

That's challenging counsel in a world that too often celebrates the ugly, evil, and banal. When I find myself in a negative slump, unable to shake off the compulsion to catalog and criticize offenses I see all around me, nothing frees me faster than sharing God's love. It can be a small sacrifice of service—bringing a meal to a friend's family even as I scramble to find the time to feed my own or hosting dinner guests when my introverted personality craves solitude. It can be a slight course correction, as when I restart a rushed and rocky homeschool morning by taking the time to discuss the Gospel of the day with my children or interrupt a chaotic lunchtime to pray the Angelus. Sometimes I have more dramatic opportunities, as when I find myself standing onstage before a thousand people talking about how much Jesus loves us and I realize, as I speak those words, how much I needed to hear them again myself.

There's something about God's love that simply can't breathe unless we share it with others. And the more we share it, the more His joy floods our hearts.

It's a funny thing about the joy of the Lord: He wants us to fling our hearts wide open to Him. But some days all we can manage is a hairline crack. And He's willing to use even that to surprise us with His joy when we least expect or deserve it.

I was reminded of that truth a couple of years ago when my family and I were visiting the hometown of Teresa of Ávila, a favorite saint of mine who was also a favorite of Francis and Angélique. The University of Ávila had invited me to keynote an international conference on Teresa to coincide with the five-hundredth anniversary of her birth. My first answer had been a reluctant no—how could I leave four preschool-aged children at home to travel to Spain?—but when the university found a sponsor to pay for John and the kids to join me, I happily reconsidered.

John and I had seen Ávila years earlier, but only for a few hours on a whirlwind trip, so we relished the opportunity to return with our children. I was eager to take a closer look at sights I had barely glimpsed the first time around, especially the dazzling, gold-bedecked Chapel of the Transverberation, where Teresa experienced a bittersweet rapture in which she felt her heart pierced with the flaming sword of God's love. This "caressing of love so sweet," as Teresa described it, was such a pivotal moment in her life and the life of her Carmelite order that it claimed its own feast day and inspired Gian Lorenzo Bernini's breathtaking sculpture, *The Ecstasy of Saint Teresa*.

Ever since I first saw that sculpture in Rome in my early twenties, I had wanted to spend some quality time in the chapel where Teresa tasted such joy. Seventeen years and four kids later, I got my chance.

We arrived in Ávila in late July 2015 and spent more than a week exploring every nook and cranny of that beautiful medieval city. We ate in its cafés, scampered across its plazas and playgrounds, and walked on top of its historic walls. We saw a lot of Teresa—her birthplace, her parish church, her monasteries, even her ring finger, severed after her death and displayed to the fascination of my five-year-old twins. And near the end of our stay, after I had delivered my big speech, we trekked down to the Monastery of the Incarnation to see the Chapel of the Transverberation.

It was supposed to be an easy jaunt; that's how I remembered it from before. But nothing is easy when you're traveling with four children ages five and under. Especially when you're jet-lagged and you've spent a week sleeping on a too-short twin bed without air-conditioning. In the middle of a heat wave. In a town where everyone else is waking up from siesta just as your family is settling in for dinner and a good night's sleep.

We were tired and cranky by the time we stepped across the threshold of Teresa's monastery that afternoon, our shirts drenched with sweat and our cheeks pink from the scorching Castilian sun. My husband and I had been taking turns toting our eighteen-month-old son through Ávila's stroller-unfriendly cobblestone streets for nearly a week by that point, and both our backs ached. I had that dull headache I always get after a major speech, no matter how well it goes. I was looking forward to slumping into a back pew and soaking up the chapel's beauty in silence.

Then I heard the music. And my heart sank.

It was singing and strumming—jubilant and loud, very loud. We turned the corner to the chapel and found a throng of Spanish young adults crooning and swaying through a particularly boisterous charismatic Mass. My children were intrigued. I might have been, too, had I gotten more sleep. Instead, I was annoyed. My interior rant began.

Why do these people have to take over the chapel with a kooky liturgy on the one day we come to visit? Do they even know what this place is? Guess we'll just have to wait until they're through. It's a shame there's so little reverence in European churches nowadays.

We spent the next hour meandering through the monastery and its museum. When it was ready to close, we returned to the chapel.

The youth Mass was still going. Only now, they weren't just rocking it out in song. They were dancing: arms linked, heads bobbing, legs kicking in the air as they circled the perimeter of the chapel where I had hoped to pray in peace.

Oh, for Pete's sake. How long is this going to last?

I was debating whether to snap a few photos of the chapel's altar or just flee when some young women in the group began motioning for us to join in. I tried to beg off, mixing mangled Spanish with some backward steps and apologetic smiles. They paid no heed. They just kept dancing and stretching their hands toward us, opening a space in their circle that they wanted us to fill.

I looked at John, who smiled, and down at my bedraggled crew of sweaty children, who looked back at me with a mix of curiosity and alarm.

I shrugged.

Then smiled.

And the next thing I knew we were dancing—all six of us, including baby Joseph in John's arms—with hearts racing and grins plastered on our flushed faces.

I didn't know the Spanish song they were singing as the recessional for this unusual Mass. But as we swayed arm-in-arm through that chapel where Teresa once drank so deeply of the joy of the Lord, I knew the One who had inspired it.

"They're dancing for Jesus," my five-year-old Maryrose yelped between breaths, as she squeezed my hand and did her best to keep time with the lively beat. "We're all dancing for Jesus!"

We were. It was beautiful—hands down, my favorite memory

of the trip. And if I'd listened to my inner critic, that sour spiritual elitist who can always find something to dislike in the Church or her fellow Christians, I would have missed it.

What's more, my children would have missed the chance to learn that even those who love the Lord in ways that seem odd or unfamiliar to us are our brothers and sisters in Christ, conduits of joy in a world where we need all the friends we can get.

A few hours after we left the monastery, while back in Ávila crisscrossing its cobblestone streets, we turned a corner and heard a shout rise up. It was that same group of young men and women, now clapping at the sight of us. It happened again an hour after that. For the rest of the day, it seemed, every other time we turned a corner in the City of Stones and Saints, our new friends were there, cheering and serenading the little foreign family that had danced with them before the Lord.

4

BRAVING THE WAVES

There is no fear in love, but perfect love drives out fear
because fear has to do with punishment,
and so one who fears is not yet perfect in love.

(1 John 4:18)

I love the ocean. Always have. Standing on the edge of the sea or splashing in its white-foam waves fills me with desire and daring. There's something about that infinite blue horizon that makes me believe I can go anywhere, do anything, be anyone. It sets my soul free.

I first fell in love with the ocean as a little girl. I was five when my father took a new job in Florida, the land of endless beaches, and brought my nine-year-old brother and me with him. My mother stayed behind in Indiana. She needed to wait for our old house to sell, my parents said, and as soon it did, she'd quit her job and join us in Florida.

What was billed as a brief separation wound up lasting nine

months. And I wound up spending my entire first-grade year with my mother nearly a thousand miles away.

My memories of that time are mostly fragments. I remember the crunch of pecans underfoot as I ran from the neighbor boy who liked to chase me under the moss-covered trees in my front yard. I see the dusty floor where I squatted with swarms of other kids in the dark home down a dirt road where my father brought me when he ran out of better babysitting options. And I feel the sunbeams that flooded my bedroom in the early evenings, warming my back as I lay facedown, weeping for my mommy.

There are happier memories, too—a few. They all involve the ocean.

Although our new home wasn't on the coast, Tallahassee is within striking distance of scores of beautiful beaches. I think we saw them all that year. My father's job required him to travel the state advocating for the rights of people with intellectual and developmental disabilities, and after suffering one too many subpar babysitters, he started taking my brother and me with him.

We'd draw or read or daydream through his morning meetings, then hit the beach with him in the afternoon. My father would toss us in the waves for hours and we'd squeal and splash to our heart's content. Dad seemed as carefree as we were in that water, his stresses and sometimes scary temper left ashore as he frolicked with us in his faded red swim trunks, his face ruddy with sun and joy. In all my childhood, I can't remember anything more fun.

We loved any beach, but the nearby Atlantic coast beaches with the most powerful surf—St. Augustine and Daytona—were my favorites. The bigger the waves, the better. I don't think my dad ever saw danger in the water or he wouldn't have let us run so free. My mom had a better sense of the risks; once she moved to Florida, my ocean play was more supervised. She often reminded her "fish" not to go out too far lest I drown.

I almost did anyway. I remember several times when the ocean's power overwhelmed me, when one rollicking wave after another hurtled me upside down, pummeled me into the sand, and then flung me back into a churn of water so violent that I couldn't tell which direction was up and I felt sure I would run out of breath.

Thankfully, I found my way back to the surface each time. I would gulp furiously at the fresh air, thank God I survived, and cast a furtive glance at shore. If my parents were none the wiser, I'd grin and go back to braving the surf.

That feeling of exhilaration and freedom returns to me every time I see the ocean. I have been known to drive hundreds of miles out of my way to soak up its perilous beauty, to spend a few moments breathing the salty sea air and wading into the pounding surf.

The ocean draws me out of myself. When I am standing before its grandeur, and even its danger, I feel closer to God. I feel like I am who I was meant to be.

That's how I used to feel, anyway. I still do, sometimes.

Beach trips are different now that I'm a mother, though. Now I am that worried parent on the shoreline, the one pleading with her children not to venture out too far. Sometimes I'm also the parent tossing tykes into the water. But only if the water isn't too cold and the waves aren't too high, if John can watch the little ones who should stay closer to shore, and if I'm not too tired from unpacking suitcases or folding laundry or rising for that early-morning run that marks my only chance all day to behold the beach in peace.

John and I recently returned from a trip to Florida's Panhandle with the kids. It was a great vacation: We rented a house across the street from the beach; we spent each day playing in the bathtub-warm turquoise waters of the Gulf; and we made the twelve-hour drive there and back from St. Louis without incident.

Of course, we also returned exhausted. The planning, the packing, the entertaining of four young children on an all-day road trip (sans videos, which we don't do)—it's a lot. Then there's the beach-day drill: swimsuits on, apocalyptic amounts of sunscreen applied, round after round of potty breaks and sandal hunts and feuds over who gets to carry the boogie boards. By the time our caravan of kids and gear lands at the beach, I'm ready for a break.

But as I sink my toes into the sand and take my first deep breath of sea air, I look up to see that my seven-year-old twins are floating halfway to Cancún on the inner tube. Then I notice that the tide is sweeping five-year-old Clara and her inflatable blue dolphin downshore at an alarming rate. And there goes three-year-old Joseph, chasing a seagull up the beach in the opposite direction, at a clip so swift he'll reach Alabama soon if I don't nab him.

So I drop my Zen beach routine and swing into action. John does the same. And we spend the rest of the day running, rescuing, refereeing, amusing, toting, and consoling. We take a noon-time break for showers, lunch, and the little one's naptime. Then we suit up and do it all again. Then more showers and meals. Rinse and repeat.

We make memories. We share laughs. Come bedtime, we crash.

We're blessed to be able to take beach vacations; some families can't. We're blessed to have children to chase; I remember how sad I was when I didn't.

Still, it's a little dispiriting to return from vacation even wearier than when you left, to look up after a week at the beach and realize you spent only a handful of minutes savoring what you waited all summer or all year to see.

It's also unsettling to notice that the carefree girl who once delighted in braving the big waves now spends her beach time fretting over jellyfish and riptides, late bedtimes and hidden sun damage, and those mounds of worries about life back home that now follow me everywhere I go, even on vacation, even into the water.

Sometimes they are little fears and questions, nibbling at my mind like the fish that nibble my toes in the deep: *Should we head back for lunch soon so we don't blow naptime or am I being too rigid? Did I handle that last kiddie meltdown the right way or was I too harsh? Can I slip away for some alone time after dinner or will John resent it? Is it his turn or mine? Am I selfish for wishing this vacation wasn't so much work? Is God angry at my ingratitude?*

Sometimes the fears and questions are bigger, the same ones that play in a loop wherever I go: *Are we living in the right place? Is this where God wants us to settle for good? Are the children getting what they need from me? Am I sacrificing enough? Too much? Am I writing what God wants me to write? Does He even want me writing at all anymore, given how hard it is to find the time? Why do I feel so tired and unsatisfied some days? So many other moms seem more serene or resigned than me. Are they secretly struggling, too? Or is it just me?*

John and I have been mulling some major decisions in recent

months. Whenever we make any progress toward pursuing long-held dreams for our life together, I feel that millstone of fear swing back around my neck. *Whoa, slow down there, sister. That's a big gamble. Might be a mistake. What will people say if you fail? Don't count on God bailing you out; you might be confusing your will for His. Better sit tight and wait for a sign. Better yet, just err on the safe side and say no.*

To hear my scaredy-cat internal monologue, you'd never know I'm the same woman who has shared my intimate struggles onstage before thousands, debated hot-button issues on cable television before millions, and sat face-to-face with the leader of the free world defending the words I wrote for him to speak. I'm an introvert and I mind my manners, most of the time. Yet I'm also outgoing at parties, almost always up for the tougher hike or longer climb, and comfortable being the only—or most outspoken—woman in a room full of powerful men.

Fear, shame, self-doubt, scrupulosity, risk avoidance—those aren't my issues.

At least, I never thought they were.

Then I started delving more deeply into this perfectionist business. And I discovered that fear plays a larger role than I realized in a host of my symptoms: that paralysis I feel when it's time to make important choices; that guilt that engulfs me when I'm longing for something others tell me I don't need or shouldn't want; that sneaking suspicion I have whenever I mess up that God can't wait to make me pay for my mistakes.

Where did I get that vindictive image of God? What does it have to do with my hunger for the approval of others and dread of their disapproval? How do I uproot fears that have burrowed so far into my psyche and soul that I barely notice them anymore, much less question their validity? And if I do question those fears—if God isn't up there manipulating and threatening me and the people telling me to simmer down and settle for less aren't actually channeling His voice—then what *is* God doing, especially in those hazy times when I'm seeking His will and He answers only with silence? How much freedom do I have to make my own decisions and follow my own desires when God's will is unclear?

In other words, is God always the one urging me to cleave to shore and play it safe?

Or is God the one daring me to come play in the waves?

When I take my questions to Scripture, one answer at least is clear:

Fear is not of God.

Over and over in the Bible, from the Book of Genesis to the Book of Revelation and nearly everywhere in between, God tells us not to fear. Jesus says it nearly twenty times in the Gospels. Paul's letters repeatedly stress that God is on the side of freedom, not fear. Even in a Bible book nicknamed the Apocalypse and focused on the terrifying battle between good and evil, the Lord reminds us twice, "Do not be afraid" (Rev. 1:17, 2:10).

The God of the Bible is fearsome in His power and jealous of His honor. Yet He is also relentless in His efforts to dispel the fear that separates our hearts from His.

We see this from the first light of Genesis, when God loves the world and our first parents into being. Adam and Eve begin life "naked, yet they felt no shame" (Gen. 2:25). Shame—and its root cause, the fear of being judged unworthy of love—only comes later, when Satan and sin arrive on the scene. Suddenly Adam and Eve are diving for the bushes to dodge God. "I heard You in the garden," Adam admits, "but I was afraid, because I was naked, so I hid" (Gen. 3:10).

Adam's fear arises from legitimate guilt over his disobedience. Sometimes ours does, too. But fear and shame are also vestiges of the original sin we inherited from our first parents, that temptation to always expect the worst of others, ourselves, and God. While healthy fear of God—known as wonder—fosters humility and repentance, this servile fear jumbles our thoughts, burdens our hearts, and strangles our freedom, all while convincing us to run from the only One who can offer us relief.

That fear is not of God. That's never of God. And when we are caught in its grip, we should bind the evil spirit of fear in the name of Jesus Christ—out loud if possible—and command it to go straight to the feet of Jesus, never to return to us or anyone else again.

Phew. That solves that.

Or does it?

Praying for deliverance from fear is a crucial step for spiritual perfectionists. But before we can seek freedom, we must recognize we are bound. That's often the harder step. Fear is a sneaky demon; it wears many disguises. And sometimes the religious voices we turn to for clarity and support only make us feel more afraid, embarrassed, and alone.

I was reminded of that some months ago, when I was having a rough week. No one was dying or diagnosed with dementia. I was simply overbooked and overwhelmed, exhausted from too little sleep and prayer time, and from solo parenting for a week while John was on call at the hospital. I was also feeling doubts about our recent move back to St. Louis, fearing we'd made a mistake, and missing the high-profile career I had put on the back burner to homeschool.

In my floundering, I opened up to a few people of faith. The wrong people, as it turned out.

The first one answered my questions with a question: "Isn't being a good mother enough for you, Colleen?" If you've ever been on the receiving end of this query, you know there's only one right answer to it. Which meant my feelings that day—that motherhood is not always enough—were wrong. And I was wrong for having them.

The next person reminded me that Jesus was nailed to a cross, so unless I can say the same, I have no business complaining. Then he told me about a woman with twice as many children as me who was doing fine, thanks to good prayer habits and daily Mass. Now I wasn't just an overwhelmed mom having a bad week. I was a whiny slacker having a bad week, and my troubles had to clear the bar of crucifixion to merit mention.

On and on it went: Are you praying about this? (Yes, all the time, thanks.) Maybe God is trying to teach you a lesson; you should trust Him more. (Maybe so, but it's hard to trust God if I picture Him as a sadistic schoolmarm using pain to smack me into shape.) That meaningful work you miss? That's a temptation, something frivolous and worldly. (OK, but before I had children, you called it a crucial, kingdom-building use of my God-given talents—so which is it?) Then there's the advice I've chafed at since I first heard it during my years-long bout with infertility: Don't try to change your situation; accept that wherever you are, whatever is happening to you, is God's will. (Really? Then why do we pray "Thy will be done" if God's will is already being done, automatically, without any effort on our part?)

The only person who said anything helpful that week was a believing-if-not-particularly-pious older woman who simply curbed her judgment long enough to listen. Her response: You're not crazy. Your feelings make sense. And if your gut says you need to make some changes, pay attention.

I wasn't sure I needed to make changes. I just wanted to be heard, to feel less alone. And while there were nuggets of truth in other counsels I received that week—suffering can be redemptive; my problems are minor compared to most; nothing happens without God's permission—most of the faith-based advice I heard only intensified my shame, sadness, and isolation.

I wish I could say I've never made anyone feel that way when they've come to me for support. Alas, I probably have. We Christians mean well. But there's more than a trace of judgment, stoicism, and fatalism running through the platitudes we spout at each other in tough times. Beneath them is fear: the fear that if we get too real with God and each other, we may be exposed as less than the rock-ribbed Christian soldiers we think we're supposed to be. We may even discover that God doesn't love us as unconditionally as we'd hoped.

Saint Alphonsus Liguori knew that fear well. From a young age, he was steeped in a religious worldview that stressed God's judgment over His mercy, one heavy on shame, blame, and terror. Yet this guilt-plagued perfectionist grew into a saint of towering courage, a celebrated bishop, writer, religious founder, and Doctor of the Church credited with singlehandedly restoring mercy and balance to Catholic moral theology.

The story of how that happened—how Alphonsus became the man that Pope Saint John Paul II described as "a gigantic figure" on par with Augustine—is as unlikely as it is inspiring. Even more compelling are the lessons that Alphonsus learned along the way, about the folly of fear-based religion and the love that alone can set us free.

Having a perfectionist parent doesn't guarantee you'll be a perfectionist, but it increases your odds—just as having a scrupulous parent makes you more likely to develop scrupulosity, a phobia of sin that leads to obsessive focus on small faults. Poor Alphonsus had parents with both traits. Given that he was also the oldest of eight children and the locus of all his family's future hopes, it's not surprising that this sensitive, artistic child became an anxious overachiever terrified of failure.

The roots of that terror can be traced partly to Alphonsus' father, Giuseppe Liguori, a harsh and domineering naval captain who chased pirates, managed slaves, and made his sons sleep on the wooden floor once a week to toughen them up. From the day Alphonsus was born in Naples in 1696, Giuseppe pushed him, hard. And Alphonsus responded by pushing himself.

That drive is how Alphonsus became a virtuoso on the harpsichord by age twelve—that, and his father's habit of locking him in a room with his music teacher for three hours at a stretch. It's how he graduated with dual degrees in civil and canon law at age sixteen, so buried in his doctoral gown that people snickered as the homeschooled child prodigy processed past. And it's how he became a celebrated attorney with his own set of professional commandments. Among them: Never take a morally murky case and pay damages for any case lost through your negligence.

His high standards, strenuous work ethic, and reputation as a dapper, cultured bachelor put Alphonsus in demand among the ladies as well as legal clients. He was, as biographer Théodule Rey-Mermet put it, "a perfect young lawyer."

Perfection has its price. Alphonsus paid his in severe scrupulosity, the religious equivalent of obsessive-compulsive disorder that turns its victims into moral hypochondriacs. While not every case of scruples is so intense—some scrupulous people have only mild or temporary experiences of this ultra-sensitivity to sin—Alphonsus was on the extreme end of the spectrum. He anguished over any flaw he found in himself and confessed the same instances of sin again and again, worried that absolution didn't "take" the first time. His fear of sexual sin was especially acute: He avoided eye contact with women, took off his glasses at the opera to avoid seeing the beauties onstage, and tied his hands in a bag before sleeping, lest he accidentally touch himself impurely.

Most biographers think Alphonsus inherited his neurotic tendencies from his mother, Anna Cavalieri Liguori, who suffered intensely from scruples herself. Anna's faith was deep and sincere; Alphonsus credited her with "all the good I have done in my childhood and the evil I have not done" and used a book of handwritten prayers that she gave him as a child until his death. Her spirituality had a severe bent, though. Anna was raised in a convent and determined to live like a nun even amid her children, treating them as mini-monastics and enforcing a devotional regimen more suited to the cloister than a boisterous family home.

As if a scrupulous mother and controlling father weren't enough to unnerve Alphonsus, there was the dysfunctional religious scene in his hometown. Some priests flouted their riches and mistresses. Others preached only hellfire and brimstone. Examples of healthy, balanced spirituality were rare, and it seemed that the only religious voices Alphonsus could trust were the extremist ones that aggravated his terror of sin. The surfeit of condemning or compromised clergy also made Naples a tough place to discern a priestly vocation, which Alphonsus was attempting to do—unbeknownst to Giuseppe, who was working hard to marry him off to the richest, well-bred bride he could find.

The inevitable crisis came in 1723, when twenty-six-year-old Alphonsus lost a high-profile court case. It was his first defeat in eight years of practicing law. A popular story holds that he overlooked a key document upon which the case turned. Biographers say Alphonsus actually knew about the document but didn't mention it because it had no legal bearing on the dispute—a judgment later confirmed by another ruling in a related case.

Alphonsus may have had logic and the law on his side, but he didn't have a judge in his pocket. When the rigged ruling came down, he was stunned, humiliated, and disgusted with the system. He locked himself in his room and refused to eat for three days, while his mother begged him to relent and his father told her to "let him die." It was an ugly scene. Things at home only got uglier when Alphonsus came out of his room. He dismissed his legal clients, broke off ties with his card-playing pals, and started spending all his time in church and volunteering at a local hospital, to the angry dismay of his social-climber father.

Not long afterward, while serving in the hospital, Alphonsus heard the distinct call from God that he had been waiting for, a voice in his heart asking him to "leave the world and give yourself to Me." Alphonsus headed straight to the Church of the Redemption of the Captives, knelt before the statue of Our Lady of Mercy, and placed his sword at her feet, a symbol of his decisive "yes" to the Lord.

The choice enraged his father. While the rest of Naples derided the lawyer-turned-seminarian as a sore loser and laughingstock, Giuseppe hollered at Alphonsus, recruited priests and monks to discourage his vocation, and refused to spring for his son's cassock or attend his vesting ceremony. "I pray God to remove me from this world or to remove you," Giuseppe sneered, on seeing Alphonsus in the dingy, used cassock he had scrounged up, "for I can no longer bear to look at you."

It was the full-throated condemnation that Alphonsus had always feared, the naked rejection he had worked all his life to avoid. Yet Alphonsus stood his ground. He had found liberation in his professional failure, a first taste of freedom to pursue the dreams of another Father whose vision for his life was grander than anything Giuseppe had in mind.

The decision to buck his father's plans and carve out his own future with God marked the start of a new life for Alphonsus. But his battle against fear had only begun.

The next test came in seminary. Alphonsus and his fellow priests-to-be studied theology from a textbook that pushed rigorism, the doctrine that when in doubt about a moral decision, you must always choose the strictest course of action.

Rigorism sounds fine in theory: Err on the ethical safe side, favor the law over liberty, avoid even the slightest appearance or possibility of sin. In practice, it's a recipe for disaster—particularly for a scrupulous perfectionist like Alphonsus.

Alphonsus already worried that feeling tempted to sin was as bad as committing sin and feeling an inspiration to do something good obligated him, under pain of sin, to follow through. Now he had a moral theory seconding his neurotic imaginings. His anxiety soon spiraled out of control, spurring a health breakdown severe enough to warrant last rites.

Alphonsus recovered and was ordained a priest in 1726, a few days shy of his thirtieth birthday. Yet his nerves remained fragile and his scruples only intensified. Now free to pursue penances without parental supervision, Alphonsus embarked on severe fasts, wore a hair shirt and stones in his shoes, ate in a kneeling posture, and used a chain to scourge himself until he bled.

None of his self-punishment alleviated his moral panic. Alphonsus had drafted a list of nine reference points for his priestly life, starting with the declaration that as a priest, his dignity "surpasses that of the angels," so he must "live an angelic life." Anything short of that standard led to crushing guilt.

Doubts and anguish would seize Alphonsus as he was preparing to celebrate Mass or receive Holy Communion or offer absolution to a penitent. Their causes ran the gamut from shame over past sins already confessed to fear of future ones and horror at bad thoughts he couldn't control.

Thankfully, Alphonsus had a wise spiritual director, Father Thomas Pagano, who set strict rules for him during this time. Among them: no repeating daily prayers you've already said even if you said them distractedly; no skipping Communion because you had a sexually explicit dream; no traipsing across town in bad weather or bad health to get to Eucharistic exposition, just pray before the tabernacle in the nearest church on those days. And no more confessing past sins or allowing scruples to disrupt your duties. If you're stuck trying to make a choice, Pagano said, "Act without worrying about the doubt, and without discussion."

Alphonsus obeyed. He wrote Pagano's advice in a little notebook that he carried with him and referred to whenever he was in doubt, which was often.

Little by little, his scruples began to recede. Alphonsus learned to recognize obsessive thought patterns as they struck and reach out to trustworthy people to test his doubts and guilt pangs before they threw him into panic. He learned to act when duty demanded it, making the best choice he could while trusting God to bring good even out of his mistakes.

Most important, Alphonsus learned that scrupulosity is not a fast-track to holiness but a do-it-yourself detour, one driven by pride as well as fear. He realized that there's a certain arrogance in assuming you know better than Christ and His Church what constitutes sin or whether forgiveness is real. There's vanity in focusing so intensely on your own spiritual concerns that you're too distracted to notice God's. Curbing that pride and fear is tough, Alphonsus would later say, but if we trust God and cooperate with His grace, scruples can become "the chisel with which God carves His statues for heaven."

Trust doesn't come easy to the scrupulous soul, of course. Even as his phobia of sin loosened its grip, Alphonsus remained oppressed by a servile fear of God.

Bishop Tommaso Falcoia, with whom he would later found the Redemptorist Order, noticed that fear shortly after meeting Alphonsus in 1732. Falcoia suspected that a distorted image of God was the problem. Was it any wonder Alphonsus was crippled by fear when he worshipped a Heavenly Father every bit as demanding, volatile, and vengeful as his earthly one? Falcoia challenged Alphonsus to rethink his view of God, to model it not on Giuseppe but on Jesus and the loving Father He reveals in the Gospels.

Alphonsus took the challenge. He immersed himself in God's Word, filling his notebook with reassuring verses about the Lord's unconditional love. He read and reread the love-saturated Song of Songs until it became a favorite Bible book. And he focused his prayers and writings on the humanity and tender approachability of Jesus, the Word-made-flesh.

Over the course of the eleven years Alphonsus spent under Falcoia's direction, love gradually replaced fear as the driving force in his faith. He came to see the return of love for love—and not the white-knuckled flawlessness of the scrupulous—as the key to Christian perfection. "Our whole perfection," he wrote, "consists in loving God who is so deserving of our love."

Alphonsus still practiced self-denial and dodged even small sins. He believed we should feel remorse whenever we offend God and stressed our duty to cooperate with grace through prayer, penance, and good works. Yet he no longer saw value in torturing himself over the sort of minor weaknesses—"distractions at prayer, useless chatter, idle curiosity, a desire to shine, choosiness in eating or drinking, the first stirrings of [illicit] sexual pleasure"—that once triggered intense anxiety.

"Although they are certainly faults," Alphonsus said, "they do not hinder us from perfection, or rather, from walking the road that leads to perfection, for no one is ever perfect until the person reaches the Kingdom of Heaven."

The truth that freed Alphonsus—that Jesus came to save us, not scare us—soon reverberated through his priestly ministry. At a time when terror-inspiring sermons were the rule and rigorist confessors often refused absolution, Alphonsus led with God's love. It's a love, he would tell his flock, as intimate as a newborn in a manger, as tangible as nail-pierced hands, as humble as a little white Host locked in a monstrance, waiting night and day for our visit.

That message resonated with Catholics hungry for hope in a time of gloom and growing religious indifference. Crowds flocked to his parish missions, kept him in the confessional for hours, and raved about his books and sermons, which brought lofty theology down to their level. By the end of his sixty years as a priest, Alphonsus had blended remarkably fruitful missionary preaching among the poor with a literary output that ranked him among the most widely read authors in history, with 21,500 editions of his books now available in seventy-two languages.

Not everyone appreciated Alphonsus. Jansenists abhorred his emphasis on the "plentiful redemption" found in Christ, which was the motto of his Redemptorist priests. The rigorists accused Alphonsus of going soft after he developed a new moral system to replace theirs, one that stressed the importance of human freedom in making moral choices when there are reasonable arguments on both sides and no clear obligations to follow the stricter course.

Alphonsus came back swinging, reminding critics that he had been one of them until reality mugged him as a young priest. One the few things that could rouse his ire was discovering that penitents were being treated harshly in the confessional. Even at the end of his life, when Alphonsus was deaf, blind, bent in half by arthritis, and suffering the betrayal of his closest confidants in the Redemptorist order, his anger was reserved for priests who failed to convey God's mercy. Hearing of one with Jansenist tendencies, the sickly and near-death Alphonsus thundered, "Tell him from me: Do not maltreat souls redeemed by the blood of Jesus Christ."

While Alphonsus suffered more than his share of attacks, his views ultimately prevailed. His capstone book, *Moral Theology*, was personally approved by the pope and became the standard text for seminarians, replacing the rigorist one he had studied in seminary. His success at forging a middle path between legalism and laxity garnered Alphonsus the unique honor of being the only moral theologian whose opinions the Catholic Church has said confessors may follow without hesitation or further consideration.

Alphonsus never lost his delicate conscience; scruples resurfaced near the end of his life, forcing him to once again lean into God's merciful love. Nor did Alphonsus ever stop calling sinners to repent before receiving the Eucharist. His reverence for the Eucharist is precisely what led him to battle the Jansenists, whom he saw scaring sinners away from the sacraments of Confession and Communion they needed most. And it was his own struggle with scruples, plus decades of ministering to those on the Church's margins, that led him to reject rigorism. "If I must err," he said, "let it be on the side of mercy and charity, of meekness and compassion. If I must be punished in the next life, let it be for too much indulgence, rather than for excessive rigor."

The transformation God worked in Alphonsus is proof that anything is possible if we cooperate with grace. It's also a reminder that our choice to live in fear or freedom is never only about us.

Fear, like freedom, is contagious. When Alphonsus was submerged in messages of judgment, shame, and blame, he nearly drowned in fear and false guilt. When he was awakened to the depths of God's love and encouraged to cherish and protect his

God-given decision-making power, he found release. And in his freedom, Alphonsus helped free countless others.

The cycle works the same for me. If I don't deal with my fear—particularly those chronic, hidden fears that limit my liberty and corrode my hope in God—I will be just another dead weight in the world, dragging others deeper into their own abyss of fear, shame, and blame. But if I look straight at my fear and give God permission to burn through it with His love, I can be a beacon instead of an anchor. My freedom from fear can inspire others to seek the same.

I don't fancy I can control others; that illusion is one I'm working to shed as a recovering perfectionist. Still, the way I live matters beyond me. It matters first of all to my children, who are looking to me to learn who God is and whether we should serve Him in love and trust or in fear and shame. It also matters to my husband, my friends and relatives, and anyone else whose life I touch—especially on days when I'm too overwhelmed or distracted to "be a witness" and my unvarnished attitudes and assumptions are shining through for all to see.

Most of those assumptions were forged in childhood. Like Alphonsus, I need to reexamine them through adult eyes, and in light of Scripture, to see how accurate they are.

For me, that starts with reconsidering what it means to be loved. Like many Catholic kids in my post–Vatican II generation, I was told early and often that God and my parents loved me, and I believed. But I also believed I had to be a good girl to keep that love coming. And while no one ever spelled it out, I always seemed to know what that entailed: *Smile pretty. Stuff secrets and scary feelings. Make us proud.*

My parents probably would've been appalled if I had articulated that creed aloud. My mother often warned me against over-work and the black-and-white thinking to which perfectionists are prone. My father, who suffered secret bouts of scrupulosity I would only learn about decades later, always cautioned me against false guilt and told me he loved me for who I was, not what I did. When I'd list the many things I knew I should do, Dad would wave a dismissive hand. "All you gotta do is die," he'd say. "No shoulds."

Family dynamics send messages parents don't intend, though. In my family, those dynamics told me I was the mascot, the child who never gives her parents grief and always makes them proud. That was my role and I embraced it. It made me feel special, safe, and worthy of love.

It was also my role to console and advise in times of crisis, by listening to grown-up problems long before I was ready and keeping my own problems under wraps if they proved too burden-some. I learned to smile when I wanted to cry—or scream. When conflicts heated up and everyone's feelings spun out of control, my job was to stay steady, calm, and quiet.

I didn't feel that way inside. Inside I felt terrified. So I learned to pretend. And my fear went underground, only to emerge in subtler, more pernicious forms—as everything from minor scru-ples, people-pleasing, and excessive caution in decision-making to intense waves of panic, shame, and self-loathing when I found myself facing failure or humiliation and I felt as small and scared as that little girl weeping on her bed in Tallahassee.

In those moments, when fear has me by the throat, God feels very far away. His love feels like a joke. And prayer feels absurd. Why turn to the One who sees your sinfulness, foolishness, and unworthiness even more plainly than everyone else?

It's taken me many years and many tears, but I've begun to realize that the condemnation I feel in those moments is not from God. That screeching hatred for my mistakes, for my weakness, for *me*—that's not from the Savior who died to give me life. That's from the Accuser, the same Father of Lies who duped Adam and Eve in the garden. And while everything inside me rebels at the thought, what I need most in those moments is to hit my knees and plead for deliverance from fear, so I can see clearly the face of the merciful Father who is always beside me, whispering through the storm, "Fear not, I am with you" (Isa. 41:10).

One thing that helps me see God's face is digging into His Word. I've spent more time studying Scripture in recent years, as I've searched for answers about perfectionism. And the more I search the Bible on my laptop, pray over its verses in the Eucharistic adoration chapel, and hear them set to music on my morning runs, the more I understand why Alphonsus said, "There is nothing more apt to stimulate a Christian to love than the Word of God."

God's Word spurs me to love because it tells me the truth about who God is. That truth bears little resemblance to my childhood caricatures of a benevolent dictator with a mile-wide mean streak. The Father who knit me in my mother's womb, sent His Son to die for me on the cross, and sustains my every breath with His Holy Spirit is for me, not against (Rom. 8:31).

Think about that for a second. Let it sink in.

God is *for* you.

He's not rooting against you.

He's not waiting for you to screw up.

He's not itching to teach you a lesson.

He is passionately, undeniably, and irrevocably *for* you.

He may not always like or bless what you're doing. God hates sin, because it separates us from Him. But in the most fundamental and ultimate sense, the only one that counts, God is always for us. He wants what's best for us. He loves us with a love "strong as death, passion fierce as the grave . . . [that] many waters cannot quench . . . neither can floods drown" (Song of Songs 8:6–7).

One of the best biblical descriptions of God's love is found Paul's First Letter to the Corinthians. It's a favorite at weddings, one that can seem trite from overuse. But take a closer look and you'll see why Alphonsus based an entire book on these three verses—*The Practice of the Love of Jesus Christ*, which he considered his most useful work. In these verses, Paul describes a love beyond anything we can give or receive or even imagine from another human being. It's literally perfect:

> *Love is patient, love is kind. It is not jealous, it is not pompous, it is not inflated, it is not rude, it does not seek its own interests, it is not quick-tempered, it does not brood over injury, it does not rejoice over wrongdoing but rejoices with the truth. It bears all things, believes all things, hopes all things, endures all things. Love never fails (1 Cor. 13:4–8a).*

I have been blessed by much love in my life. I consider myself a loving person. But a love that is always patient and kind, that never gets jealous or seeks self or holds grudges or rejoices in wrongdoing? A love that endures *all* things? That *never* fails? Never?

There's only One who can love me like that. There's only One who can love my husband and children and family and friends and neighbors and rivals and critics like that. The perfect love that casts out fear comes from only one Source: God.

Fortunately, He's not a hoarder. The Lord wants to share His perfect love with me. And He wants to use the imperfect vessel of my heart to share it with others, too.

My job, then, is not to feign perfection or tiptoe through life trying not to make messes or mistakes. My job is to clear a path in my heart to receive the liberating gift of God's love and allow it to flow through me into the world.

I can't do that unless I'm willing to trust God even when it feels foolish or unsafe. And I can't trust God if I don't know Him and let Him know me, if I try to hide from Him what I really want, how I really feel, and who I really am.

God doesn't love me only when I'm wearing my good girl dress. He doesn't value me only when I put on my brave face. God loves me always and everywhere—no conditions, no exceptions, no blackout dates.

If I believe that, really believe it, I don't need to be a slave to fear. Ever. Not even when I sin.

I need to seek forgiveness. But I don't need to keep my distance. Instead, I need to run to God's arms and beg for a dunk in His ocean of mercy. I need to recover the trust of that little girl who felt so fearless when being tossed in the waves by her daddy.

"For you did not receive a spirit of slavery to fall back into fear," Paul writes, "but you received a spirit of adoption, through which we cry, 'Abba [Daddy], Father!'" (Rom. 8:15).

God is my loving Father, my Daddy. That makes me a beloved daughter of the King, a woman born to live free.

So what does that look like in daily life, to live free from fear?

In my life, it looks like knees on the ground first thing in the morning and a whispered prayer for deliverance from fear, anxiety, shame, blame, and false guilt. As I move through my day, it means watching for that telltale tightening in my chest, chill in my palms, or chorus of accusations in my head that signal fear is taking control. It means buying time when someone makes a request that I'm tempted to agree to because I want to please or impress or avoid conflict. It means asking questions and searching for alternatives when I feel trapped in a situation with no good options and no way out. It means guarding against my own tendencies to blame, shame, or judge others when I'm feeling cornered or panicked. And it means admitting and confessing when I fail, but not punishing myself for past mistakes.

In my decision-making, living free from fear means seeking the counsel of Spirit-filled, prayerful people whose lives prove their willingness to radically trust God, and tuning out those who always make me feel silly or stupid or bad or wrong. It means no longer defaulting to the safe or smart choice, or to the hardest or strictest option.

I still must watch and pray for signs of God's will. Choices that contradict the teachings of my faith or demands of my vocation are nonstarters. But in those gray areas where there isn't a right or wrong answer and God isn't sending lightning bolts, I've come to see that He isn't abandoning me. He's respecting my freedom. God is inviting me to use my judgment and trust that wherever I go, whatever I choose, He'll be by my side.

I don't always live like this, mind you. This is how I live on my good days, and how I aspire to live on all the rest. I'd like to think I'm winning the fight against fear, but it's a new battle each day. And those days pass more swiftly than they once did.

I was reminded of that recently, when my family and I were

treated to a front-row seat at the Great American Eclipse of 2017. It was the first total solar eclipse to cross coast-to-coast in the United States in nearly a century. The seventy-mile-wide path of totality—where you could see the moon totally cover the sun—fell across our suburban St. Louis home. So we set out lawn chairs in our driveway, slapped on our ISO-approved sunglasses, and savored the eerie beauty of midnight in the middle of the day, complete with the chirping of crickets and flickering of streetlamps confused by nature's most stunning celestial trick.

The atmosphere was electric as we watched the moon inch over the sun that August afternoon. Along with millions of others, we counted down to the moment when we could pop off our glasses and stare, transfixed, at the dazzling black ball in the sky and the sun's brilliant white corona radiating around it.

The moment arrived, and it didn't disappoint. As we gawked at the wonder of God's creation in the darkened sky, I stole a glance back at our little crew. There they were: best buds John Patrick and Maryrose, foreheads still sweaty from chasing each other in the backyard all morning; their pigtailed little sister, Clara, wearing multiple shades of mismatched blue that she had carefully selected for the occasion; and baby brother, Joseph, with his impossibly pudgy cheeks and sandals that were, as usual, on the wrong feet. Behind them all stood John, smiling and strapping and strong.

As I looked at my husband and children, the thought came to me:

It's going fast.

Not only the eclipse. Our life as a young family, this stage of raising babies.

Before I know it, in years that will someday feel as fleeting as the moments it took the moon to pass across the sun, this will be over. My children will be out of my home, off on their own adventures. They'll take with them only memories—of what I said, but even more, of how I lived. And I will be left to ponder how I spent the years God gave me, as I see more of them in the rearview mirror than on the horizon.

When I look back over my life, will I be racked with regret over countless hours wasted on fear, worry, and indecision, on playing games with God and guilt trips on myself? Or will I be filled with gratitude at how God cared for me as I took bold risks to follow my dreams and answer His call?

Will I wish I had spent more time playing it safe? Or more time dancing in the waves?

I know how I want to live, how I want my children to see me living. And that means I have no more time for fear. I've wasted too much already.

"It is for freedom that Christ set us free," Paul says. "Stand firm, then, and do not let yourself be burdened again by a yoke of slavery" (Gal 5:1).

It may take many more days of struggle, but I'm determined to break free of fear.

For me, for my children, for God.

And for good.

5

THE WAR WITHIN

Do not be conformed to this world,
but be transformed by the renewal of your mind,
that by testing you may discern what is the will of God,
what is good and acceptable and perfect.

(Rom. 12:2)

Baby number four was a game-changer for me.

After a frantic pregnancy spent balancing nonstop nausea with an interstate move, care of three preschoolers, and a new, full-time TV anchor-producer job that was supposed to have been part-time, I stumbled into maternity leave desperate for down time. But once I got it, with the birth of my son Joseph in early 2014, the transition was jarring.

As I nursed my newborn hour after quiet hour in the isolation of a house I still hadn't unpacked, the full force of my accumulated weariness and disillusionment bore down on me. I had moved my family across the country for a dream job that wasn't—

a job that both John and I had believed God wanted me to take. I had weathered a season of gale-force stress only to find myself suffocating in an eerie, post-partum calm. I felt like a junkie coming off a bad trip, my nerves still rattled by the big move that now looked like a big mistake.

Slowly, though, I began to catch my breath. Weeks passed, and I started praying more, reading again, remembering how much I loved simply being with my kids, with nothing more pressing than naptime on our daily agenda. I realized I had missed writing—those two-minute TV news packages hardly counted, and my five hundred–word op-eds weren't much more satisfying. I began to dream of writing new books, to collect ideas for celebrating the liturgical seasons and saint feast days at home, to look forward to exploring a new city with four little people and a cell phone that no longer screeched and buzzed all hours for my attention. I started to wonder: Could it be that this move wasn't a mistake after all, that Jesus used all this stress and disappointment at work to open my heart to a new call—one He had in mind for me all along?

For years, I had felt a growing dissatisfaction with journalism, a sense that even in my turn from secular to religious media, I was often doing little more than adding to the world's noise, albeit with a Christian accent. In the fallow season of my maternity leave, God hardened that hunch into a conviction. I sensed a call to trade the higher-profile, chase-the-pack media work that impressed others for the deeper, more demanding creative work that attracted me: the work of educating my children and writing books that could change lives, not just minds.

The prospect filled me with joy. Fear, too—I'd harbored a longstanding phobia about sacrificing my career to kids, and the term "homeschooling mother" still conjured images of a mousy haus frau who makes her own soap and sports the same denim jumper as her fourteen crocheting, cow-milking daughters. But after cold-calling a dozen or so D.C.-area homeschool moms and discovering what a diverse, savvy, and smart bunch they were, I felt more joy than fear. I also felt sure that God wasn't asking me to surrender my writing and speaking career. He was asking me to streamline it, to let go of the frenetic media work that scattered my focus and jumbled my home life and rediscover the original passion that had seized me as a girl: a passion for creative writing that I'd shelved long ago in my quest for security and success.

So when Joseph turned two months, I quit my TV show and cleared the decks for the rest of the year, accepting only one speaking invitation and a handful of op-ed requests. I wanted a season of rest to reconnect with God, my family, and my own desires. And that fall, I began to homeschool my twins.

My first year of all-in motherhood was hard but beautiful, a luxury I know many women never have. As it drew to a close, I felt confirmed in my new path. My kids were thriving; my creative energy was back; and I felt a renewed longing to engage with readers and test my new book ideas on live audiences. I knew God wasn't calling me to rejoin the media rat race, but I sensed His nudge to return to the speaking circuit with a few select events, the kind I could do with twelve-month-old Joseph in tow. One of the first was a Catholic women's conference in Columbus, Ohio.

Getting there was tough. Joseph and I ran into one headache after another: delayed flights, snooty passengers miffed at sitting near a baby (even one quieter than most adults on the plane), and, just in time for landing, a massive snowstorm. We persevered, though, and somehow wound up arriving as scheduled at a field house packed with 1,500 hearty Midwesterners who weren't about to let a record-setting snowfall spoil their plans.

I settled Joseph with the gaggle of veteran mamas who had promised to dote on him during my speech, then headed into the auditorium. As I stood at the podium and launched into my remarks, I felt myself relaxing for the first time in two days. I relished the spotlight's warm glare, the audience's easy laughter at my one-liners and pin-drop silence at my intimate stories. *I've missed this,* I thought. *It was a lot of trouble to get here, but they needed me and I needed them. Thank You, Jesus, for bringing me here to do this for You again.*

I was halfway through my speech, the audience and I in perfect sync, when I heard a piercing cry from the hallway. It was Joseph, wailing for me.

My forehead flushed and mind raced. *What does he need? Did I forget to change him? Did he need to nurse longer? He seemed happy when I left him. Was there an accident? Is he hurt?*

I reminded myself that the conference organizers would alert me if there was an emergency. And it wasn't as if Joseph were a newborn. By the time the twins were his age, I was leaving them with John for entire weekends on occasion so I could speak or write. Surely Joseph could survive a forty-five-minute separation from Mommy.

I forged on with the story I was telling, noticing absently that many of the women were now leaning forward in their chairs to follow along. They seemed oblivious to Joseph's wailing, but I heard it in stereo. With each cry, I felt more of my enthusiasm and gratitude slipping away. All of the discouragement and frustration I had kept at bay for the past forty-eight hours came roaring back, along with years-old angst over balancing work and family. That interior voice that only moments ago had been praising God now turned against me, violently.

Why am I still trying to do this, still dragging babies across the country to give speeches someone else could give just as well or better? It's too hard. How many more ways does God have to show me that I can't do this anymore, that I can't do anything anymore, other than motherhood? It's not enough to give up the show, the op-eds. I need to give this up, too. Probably also the books. This will never work.

I fought to maintain my focus, to remind myself that John and I had consistently heard in prayer that God still wanted me using my gifts in the wider world, albeit in a limited way. I continued speaking words of hope to the women before me and even managed a wan smile to acknowledge their standing ovation when I finished. But as I bolted offstage and through the cheering crowd, I felt only defeat. I was desperate to escape, to scoop up my baby and surrender what suddenly seemed like a foolish attempt to resume a career that would never mesh with the kind of mother I wanted to be.

Then I reached the hallway, and an odd thing happened. My discouragement evaporated.

Joseph didn't look nearly as bad as he had sounded. Within minutes, he was calm and cooing in my arms. No permanent emotional scars, nothing more than the predictable fallout of a few missed naps. I decided I could stay for a book signing, and as I glimpsed the hundred-plus women already lined up to meet me, I realized I was looking forward to it.

I sat down at my book table, Joseph grinning in my lap, and began greeting the women one by one. As they shared how my words had helped them, some with tears running down their cheeks and arms outstretched for hugs, I realized that a few minutes of panic for me and a few forgotten cries for Joseph were a small price to reach these souls for Jesus. Maybe I had made the right call in coming after all.

If so, what was that anguish onstage all about? At the time, the darkness had felt so thick and impenetrable, so much worse than a crying baby or a little jet lag warranted. A year's worth of confirmations that I was on the right track, that I could still pursue writing and speaking as a homeschooler, had seemed to vanish before my eyes. I was left with only the grim certainty that what I was doing wasn't worth the effort because it didn't matter to anyone, even God.

Now, minutes later, I felt fine.

When I was a little girl, discernment was simple: Icky feelings mean God isn't happy with where I am or what I'm doing. Good feelings mean things are OK. Following God's will isn't always easy, but if I consult the Lord when making decisions, they'll always turn out well and I'll never second-guess them.

Adulthood made quick work of my girlish assumptions. Suffering, sin, lingering confusion around issues for which I had sought God's guidance for years—my black-and-white discernment approach proved a poor match for the gray matter of grown-up life.

That didn't stop me from reverting to my childhood ideas, though, particularly in times of stress. I knew plenty about discernment in theory: that different emotions have different spiritual significance depending on the context; that discerning God's will isn't as simple as merely following the Commandments or doing what feels right. I could quote you chapter and verse about consolations—those interior experiences of closeness to God, about desolation—the experience of spiritual dryness or distance from God, and about spiritual warfare and all the rest. But under pressure, I frequently reverted to my little-girl rubric, the one that fit so neatly with my perfectionist worldview: Feeling bad means God is mad; feeling good means full steam ahead.

The Columbus speech reminded me that the time for that simplistic approach was over. The bad feelings that had tempted me to walk offstage mid-speech couldn't be equated with the bittersweet-but-fruitful maternity-leave blues that had awakened me to my latent desires for book-writing and homeschooling, any more than the fleeting thrill of a prestigious media invitation could match the deep-down joy I felt spending my days on the people and projects that mattered most. The pangs of discouragement and distraction I'd suffered with increasing frequency in recent years were not mere hassles or trials; they were temptations. And I couldn't combat them armed with only my childhood notions of discernment or intellectual knowledge I had failed to integrate. I needed to cultivate the daily habit of mature Christian discernment, to get better at figuring out which of my feelings come from God, which don't, and how to respond to each.

I once thought that paying so much attention to my feelings was self-indulgent. Don't the saints always warn us not to navelgaze? After my Columbus experience, though, I began to notice how much my ability to read and heed God's messages impacts those around me—especially John and the kids. If I'm stressed and irritable because I let momentary excitement dupe me into taking on a commitment I don't have time for, they'll soon be stressed and irritable, too. If I interpret every wave of discouragement as a divine verdict on my decision to homeschool or write books or try to combine the two, they'll feel the sting of failure as well—not to mention the misery of living with someone miserable. And if I discount those red-alert intuitions that tell me to steer clear of a person, place, or product that everyone else says is fine for my children, it isn't me who will pay the steepest price. It's them.

The same goes for all those affected by my moods, my words, and my work. Prayerful pursuit of emotional awareness helps me sidestep the devil's traps so I can do the good God wants me to do in the world, for others as well as myself. Over the span of years, the habit of bringing my feelings to Jesus each day for clarity and direction can make the difference between a life of fruitfulness and purpose and one of chaos and confusion that leads others astray, too.

Psychology can be a great help here. "Holiness is wholeness," my mom always said, when explaining how her work as a counselor and social worker related to her faith. It's true: When was the last time you met a loving, wise, and holy Christian who was completely out of touch with her emotions? Christian counselors and therapists can be great partners in helping us cultivate the emotional awareness we need for effective discernment.

But Scripture says we can't achieve self-knowledge through human effort alone. As Jeremiah laments, "The heart is deceitful above all things, beyond cure. Who can understand it?" (Jer. 17:9). Only God, the Psalmist answers:

You have searched me, Lord, and You know me. You know when I sit and when I rise; You perceive my thoughts from afar. . . . Such knowledge is too wonderful for me, too lofty for me to attain (Ps. 139:1–2, 6).

Happily, God wants to share His knowledge with us. He wants us to understand our feelings and His will, to hear His voice above the din. God doesn't give us crystal-clear answers to every question, but I think He gives more answers than most of us realize. It's in listening for them, and interpreting them, that things get tricky.

One reason they're tricky is that we have an enemy working to scramble God's messages to us. Scripture says Satan isn't only the Father of Lies (John 8:44), he's also the author of confusion (1 Cor. 14:33) who "has blinded . . . minds . . . to keep them from seeing the light of the Gospel" (2 Cor. 4:4). When assaulted by confusion, Paul says, we must "fight the good fight" (1 Tim. 1:18) using weapons that "are not of the flesh but are enormously powerful" (2 Cor. 10:4).

One the mightiest weapons is discernment. "Do not trust every spirit," John warns, "but test the spirits to see whether they belong to God" (1 John 4:1). Discernment is the means of that testing. It's the way we learn to listen to and interpret the movements of our hearts to distinguish the inspirations of the Holy Spirit from ideas that proceed merely from other people, our own pride or woundedness, or evil spirits trying to lead us astray.

That's an important skill for anyone, but it's essential for spiritual perfectionists. Perfectionism thrives in the petri dish of knee-jerk reactions, unexamined assumptions, and emotional disconnect. Our unacknowledged feelings and beliefs are the reason we do crazy things—like driving eighty-five miles an hour to a baby shower—that make no sense, even to us. Most of us can't stop doing those things until we learn to step outside the churning swirl of our emotions and prayerfully evaluate where they're coming from and where they're leading us.

Discernment enables us to do that, to imitate the serene, clearheaded example that Jesus gives us in the Gospels. While everyone around Him is mired in confusion or blown by winds of fear or flattery, Jesus judges not "by appearances" but in union "with the Father who sent Me" (John 8:15–16). He "knew in His spirit what they were thinking in their hearts" (Mark 2:8) and frequently calls out evil spirits even in His friends: "'Get behind Me, Satan! . . . You are thinking not as God does, but as human beings do'" (Matt. 16:23). Jesus sees through the devil's deceits in the desert (Matt. 4:1–11) and warns His followers to "watch and pray" (Matt. 26:41) so they can do the same. "Satan has demanded to sift all of you like wheat, but I have prayed that your faith may not fail" (Luke 22:31–32). That prayer for our spiritual defense is one of the last Jesus utters before His death: "I do not ask that You take them out of the world but that You keep them from the evil one" (John 17:15).

One way we can steer clear of the evil one is by seeking and nurturing God's gift of a discerning heart. We do that first of all through fidelity to prayer, the sacraments, and the study of Scripture. We also do it by learning from the real-time spiritual companions the Lord puts in our path: all those pastors, spiritual directors, confessors, parents, spouses, and friends whose serenity we admire and whose insights are often spot-on.

Sometimes we find ourselves between spiritual mentors, though, or struggling with a problem that Scripture doesn't spell out and even the wisest, holiest people we know don't understand. Sometimes we have no shortage of good advice but we crave a sturdier framework for understanding where that advice comes from and why it works, for making sense of why we fall into the same traps time and again and what we can do to avoid them in the future.

It would be so much easier if there were rules to follow—clear, explicit, biblically-based guidelines for understanding how the Holy Spirit tends to speak in our hearts and how Satan tends to mimic and obscure God's voice. Even better would be to learn those rules from a fellow perfectionist, someone who overcame the same toxic patterns that entangle us and once found the amorphous art of discernment as daunting as we do.

Enter Ignatius of Loyola. This sixteenth-century Spanish scallywag-turned-saint is known the world over for founding the Society of Jesus, leading a period of desperately needed Catholic renewal in the wake of the Protestant Reformation, and authoring the seminal and still popular *Spiritual Exercises*. Most important for us, Ignatius was a recovering perfectionist who drew on his Scripture-steeped faith, psychological acumen, and dirt-under-the-fingernails experience to develop nearly two dozen practical rules for discerning spirits.

Those rules, which have enlightened countless souls over the past five centuries, are still the gold standard for Christian discernment today. And for perfectionists, they are something more: a concrete reminder that the very temptations that seem destined to defeat us can become, in God's hands, a mother lode of blessing.

Given how much the Ignatian discernment method stresses emotional awareness, it's tempting to assume that its creator was a natural-born model of psychological integration, an innately placid boy encouraged from birth to explore and express his feelings.

Of course, if you know anything about how God operates—by choosing the least likely candidates for the most crucial missions—you can guess that this patron saint of emotional awareness began his life as anything but. The young Iñigo de Loyola was a tangled mess of stoicism, rage, and reckless bravado, a roguish ruffian who found himself on the wrong end of the law, and the dagger, more than once.

The youngest of thirteen children born into a noble family in Spain's Basque country, Iñigo lost his mother at his birth in 1491. He was then sent to live with the local blacksmith, whose wife nursed and raised him with her own children until he returned to his family's castle around age seven.

If leaving the only mother and family he had ever known was hard, Iñigo learned not to show it. Instead, he imitated the swagger and machismo of his father and six older brothers. Handsome and passionate, born with a double dose of the thirst for glory that drove the other Loyola men, adolescent Iñigo ate up stories of chivalry and courtly love, fussed over his looks, and gravitated to anything active or daring: fencing, riding, dueling, gambling, dancing, and romancing beautiful women—including one whose jealous boyfriend tried to kill him.

Iñigo wasn't easily intimidated. Once, when a gang of men cornered him, he drew his sword and chased them down the street, ready to kill every last one of them until peacemakers intervened. Another time he faced a serious court charge for a violent crime. Details are murky, but one story holds that Iñigo and his brother jumped some priests from a rival family during carnival time, then Iñigo escaped prosecution by pretending to be a priest-in-training.

Iñigo's appetite for risk finally caught up with him in 1521, when he was twenty-nine. He was fighting to defend the fortress of Pamplona from French invaders when a cannonball hit him between the knees, crushing the bones of his right leg and tearing open the calf of his left. The battle, like Iñigo's military career, was over.

His French captors were so impressed by his courage that they brought Iñigo to his family's castle rather than to prison. There he suffered one excruciating surgery after another. There was no anesthetic to ease his pain as doctors broke, re-set, sawed off, and stretched out his mangled bones. Iñigo silently gritted his teeth and clenched his fists, determined to suffer whatever it took to make his legs work—and look—well again.

He spent almost a year waiting for his legs to heal. Bored and sore, Iñigo asked to read some tales of courtly romance to pass the time. His pious sister-in-law, who was now running the Loyola household, was no fan of lowbrow fiction. So she gave him the only books she had: a four-volume life of Christ and a collection of stories about the saints.

Iñigo accepted them grudgingly and read them fitfully at first, between daydreams of returning to the battlefield and winning the love of beautiful women. As he read, though, something began to shift within him. Iñigo started imagining himself serving a King above all kings and chasing the sort of glory a cannonball couldn't shatter and death couldn't destroy. When he nursed these strange new desires, he felt joy—a joy that lingered even after he set his religious books and dreams aside.

It was different with his worldly daydreams. Iñigo enjoyed those, too, for a while. But as soon as they passed, he felt dry, discontent, and more dissatisfied than before. The difference caught his attention. As it says in his autobiography, which is based on memories he dictated to another writer, *he began to wonder at this difference and to reflect upon it. From experience he knew that some thoughts left him sad while others made him happy, and little by little he came to perceive the different spirits that were moving him: one coming from the devil, the other coming from God.*

Iñigo concluded that God was trying to speak to him through his feelings and that he ought to pay attention to them. So when he arose from his sickbed at age thirty, he did so as a different kind of warrior: a soldier for Christ.

Iñigo had never been a man for half measures. Once he decided to follow Christ, he did so the only way he knew: all the way.

He began by taking a 350-mile mule ride to a shrine near Barcelona, where he made an overdue visit to the confessional, left his sword and dagger at an altar dedicated to Mary, and pledged a vow of chastity before passing an entire night in prayer. Then he gave away his clothes and mule, donned a sackcloth robe, and walked fifteen more miles to the small town of Manresa, carrying only a pilgrim's staff to steady his still-swollen right leg.

Iñigo intended to spend only a few days in Manresa, enough to beg for some food before heading to Barcelona to catch a ship for the Holy Land. Instead, he wound up staying nearly a year, one that proved the most pivotal of his life. It was in Manresa that Iñigo first battled the discouragement and distraction that bedevil so many spiritual perfectionists, the very temptations that spurred him to forge his famous discernment principles.

Discouragement came first. Like many a new convert, Iñigo arrived in Manresa full of fire for his faith and shame for his sins.

He divided his time between a cave that he used as a chapel, the homes of locals willing to shelter him, and a small room in the Dominican priory where he knelt in prayer for seven hours at a stretch. Barefoot, penniless, and seized by a desire for penance, Iñigo let his hair and nails grow so long that townspeople mistook him for a wild beast. He conducted all-night prayer vigils, scourged himself with a whip, and consumed only one piece of hard black bread and a cup of water a day. On Sundays, he added a glass of wine and some herbs—but mingled with dirt, lest they taste too good.

Iñigo suffered physically in Manresa, with bouts of serious illness, and spiritually and psychologically, with doubts, dryness, anxiety, guilt, scruples, and sadness that plagued him between times of great spiritual joy. The whiplash between agony and ecstasy disoriented him and desperation for holiness consumed him. He wondered how he could sustain this intensity for the rest of his life. Wouldn't life just drag on and on? His monastery room faced a deep pit and several times while praying, Iñigo felt the urge to fling himself into it and end it all.

Iñigo resisted those impulses, but their violence caught his attention. Determined to escape his interior torments once and for all, he resolved not to eat or drink again until God gave him relief or he saw that death was near. Iñigo was well on his way to starvation when he confided his plan to his confessor. The priest ordered him to eat. Iñigo obeyed, and his torments ceased.

A few days later, Iñigo began thinking again of his past mistakes and decided to repeat the general confession of all the sins of his life that he had already made twice. Soon disgust with his life and dread about his future returned.

This time, though, something was different. As he had on

his sickbed at Loyola, Iñigo received the grace to step outside his emotions and analyze them objectively. How had he lost his peace and wound up back on the brink?

Iñigo examined the progression of his thoughts one by one. He realized that it was his decision to repeat his confession that had triggered his relapse. He decided then and there to never again confess past sins. His peace returned. And this time, his autobiography says, he knew "that our Lord in His mercy had liberated him."

After unmasking his temptation to discouragement, Iñigo changed his spiritual tact. He started taking care of himself again, moderating his penances, and guarding against the extremes of self-punishment and self-loathing to which he now knew he was prone. The changes seemed to work—until a new trap ensnared him.

Still living in Manresa and momentarily free from desolation, Iñigo began following a more balanced but still rigorous daily schedule. He prayed seven hours a day and divided the rest of his time between helping at the local hospital, reading and writing about religious matters, visiting shrines, and giving spiritual direction. When it finally came time for sleep, he lay down on bare boards or the cold ground of his cave for a few hours.

Sleep didn't come, though. Instead, night after night, Iñigo began experiencing "great illuminations and spiritual consolations" that were so profound and pleasing he couldn't stop turning them over in his mind. These pious thoughts, his autobiography says, "made him lose much of the time he had set aside for sleep, and that was not much." Iñigo would rise in the morning exhausted and poorly prepared to carry out the duties to which God had called him.

The problem puzzled the budding mystic. On the one hand, Iñigo could see that sleep deprivation was compromising his prayer life and service to others. On the other, he was staying up all night to think about God, so how could that be wrong?

Drawing on what he had first learned about discernment during his convalescence—that thoughts from God leave us joyful, not weary, dry, or restless—Iñigo took another look at his night visions. Here he was giving all his waking hours to God. Was it likely that God wanted him to forgo sleep, too? Or were those apparently holy thoughts actually a distraction intended to lead him back to the threshold of exhaustion and despair?

Iñigo realized that he was dealing with what Paul calls "an angel of light" (2 Cor. 11:14): a false consolation or apparent good that is actually a temptation in disguise. He decided to reject his nocturnal inspirations and get some sleep.

It was a small triumph but a crucial one. Iñigo was learning that, as Jesuit William Barry puts it, "God is not the only source of pious thoughts." Or as Iñigo himself later explained, "the enemy does not care whether he speaks truth or falsehood so long as he gets the better of us."

Over the next thirty-five years, as hotheaded Iñigo evolved into disciplined spiritual father Ignatius of Loyola, the lessons he learned in Manresa guided him through one trial after another. They laid the groundwork for his extraordinary success as leader of the Jesuits, equipped him to guide scores of souls to a clearer understanding of God's will, and furnished the raw material for his *Spiritual Exercises*, which continue to transform hearts and lives today.

By the time Ignatius died in 1556, a few months shy of his sixty-fifth birthday, the habit of daily, prayerful discernment that he first cultivated at Manresa had allowed him to scale the heights of mystical prayer and overcome character defects that once seemed permanent. His temptations to discouragement and distraction, his extreme penances and rash judgments, even his perfectionism itself—all were tamed and eventually conquered through discernment. As Jesuit biographer and psychiatrist W. W. Meissner writes:

> His early ascetical career had a quality of excess and fanatical inten-sity that was abnormal, if not pathological. But from circumstance and necessity, he gradually moderated these practices . . . The theme of discernment that runs throughout his mystical experience bespeaks the constant exercise of judgment, discrimination, and discretion, even during his mystical elevations.

I find reason for hope in those lines. If discernment skills can turn an impetuous, emotionally erratic character like Ignatius into a man now known as the "mystic of moods and thoughts," as Jesuit Harvey Egan describes him, then surely they can help me.

Of course, my problems are different than those of Ignatius. I'm not lying awake all night contemplating the Trinity; you'll more likely find me fretting how to get the kids to a soccer prac-tice tomorrow that starts five minutes after tumbling class ends across town. As for desolation, I've got it in spades some weeks—that shock of discouragement I felt in Columbus is now a regu-lar occurrence—but I can't blame severe penances or crippling repentance. Too often its arrival feels random, though short-changing sleep and prayer can set the stage.

Thankfully, I don't have to experience everything Ignatius did to benefit from his wisdom. The twenty-two discernment rules he mined from his Manresa experiences are a treasure trove of practical, all-purpose insights that can help anyone. I won't attempt a detailed analysis of them here—modern guides such as the series by Timothy Gallagher, O.M.V., already do that quite well—but I will highlight a few takeaways that I've found particularly helpful in my own battles with the same discouragement and distraction that almost derailed Ignatius.

The first is this: If we're walking closely with the Lord, and striving to follow His will, our bouts of discouragement and desolation aren't from Him. And as long as we're under the influence of those feelings, we shouldn't make any course corrections other than to intensify our prayer and self-denial.

Sounds simple enough, right? If the devil tries "to harass with anxiety, to afflict with sadness, to raise obstacles backed by fallacious reasonings that disturb the soul," as Ignatius describes desolation, don't give in. Step up the prayer and stay the course.

Think of the last time you felt discouraged, though. Did you want to crack open your Bible, hit the confessional, roll up your sleeves to stock shelves at the food pantry? Or did you want to snarf a bag of truffles while downloading mindless movies and whining to a friend about the latest outrage inflicted by your most obnoxious relative?

I know. You never do that sort of thing. Me neither.

Whether we admit it or not, though, desolation makes us want to do the things we shouldn't and turn away from the things of God. Consider how Ignatius describes the spiritual state of desolation (which is distinct from the psychological or medical condition of depression):

> . . . *darkness of soul, turmoil of spirit, inclination to what is low and earthly, restlessness rising from many disturbances and temptations which lead to want of faith, want of hope, want of love. The soul is wholly slothful, tepid, sad, and separated, as it were, from its Creator and Lord.*

Feeling like this isn't merely unpleasant. It can be spiritually perilous, particularly for perfectionists. If you already judge yourself and others harshly, if life doesn't measure up to your standards even on a good day, then times of desolation—when your natural bent toward discouragement, anxiety, or criticism is intensified—can feel calamitous. The all-or-nothing thinking of a perfectionist can make bleak situations look bleaker and extreme solutions seem like the only ones you've got. You can feel so desperate to escape the valley of desolation that you take drastic measures to catapult out of it—measures that usually make things worse.

Don't, Ignatius advises. Don't cancel that trip, peel off that angry email, tell off that coworker or relative who so richly deserves it. Don't surrender to self-pity and sullenness or curtail prayer time that suddenly feels pointless. Doing so only emboldens the devil to push harder. He will, Ignatius says, and if he sees that he's getting somewhere, "no wild animal on earth can be more fierce."

Instead, Ignatius says, ask God for strength, confide in a spiritual friend, and remind yourself that the Lord's consolation—those feelings of "courage and strength, consolations, tears, inspirations, and peace"—will return soon. Then get to work doing more of the things that tick off the devil: being kind to those who aren't kind to you, staying calm when all is falling apart, trusting Jesus to manage problems that you can't. Satan sends desolation "to prevent the soul from advancing," Ignatius says, but if the devil sees desolation leading you closer to God, he'll let up. And you'll emerge with a purer faith and deeper dependence on the Lord than before desolation hit—which may be the reason God allowed it in the first place.

That leads to the second key takeaway from the Ignatian rules: Desolation times can be useful. If you pay attention to when they come, the forms they take, and your response to them, these dry seasons can help you spot weaknesses in yourself that you might never otherwise discover—weak points that God and the devil have seen all along.

Now, it's tempting to think we perfectionists don't need this sort of revelation. We're always noticing and lamenting our faults. Hyper-focus on faults is our defining characteristic, after all, along with outsized shame and guilt. How could we not know our weak points?

Here's the thing, though: The devil's favorite weaknesses aren't the ones we know and worry about. He'll settle for those in a pinch, but his favorites are those we overlook while fretting over our own spiritual pet peeves. Often our weak points are the flip side of our strongest virtues, obvious to everyone but us.

Take the dependable guy with the gold-star work ethic. He may loathe the thought of letting anyone down at the office and berate himself mercilessly for that rare missed deadline. But his real weak point is his habit of neglecting prayer and his family under stress.

Or think of the self-sacrificing mother whose carefully honed caregiving and listening skills career into codependency and smothering when she's anxious. She thinks she's a martyr; to her family, her "selflessness" in these times feels suffocating and pathological.

Sometimes weak points are circumstantial. We may feel clearheaded and confident when disciplining our children but confused and timid when dealing with a boundary-crossing parent or sibling. We may hear the Holy Spirit loud and clear when dreaming up new projects, but habitually succumb to panic and dread when it's time to get to work on them.

Among perfectionists, the most common and dangerous weak point is what Jesuit author David Fleming calls the "complacent strength which is self-sufficient pride." It's that hidden conviction that we are (or ought to be) strong enough to weather desolation without God's help and see our situation clearly without His enlightenment. This pride makes perfectionists doubly frustrated in desolation—first, by our dark feelings, and then by our inability to banish them of our own power. Too often, we respond by doubling down on self-reliance and digging ourselves deeper into desolation.

The good news is that even if you're a slow learner like me, Ignatian principles can help you use desolation to learn important truths about yourself. In my case, that's meant facing the fact that I'm far more dependent on pleasant emotions, signal favors, and conspicuous graces than I like to imagine.

It's easy to believe I'm fully committed to Christ when He's sending me warm fuzzies. Even awful days, such as the one when my father died, feel manageable in the golden glow of consolation.

It's different when desolation strikes. Then I'm on my own—or, at least, it seems like I'm on my own. The bottom falls out and the smallest hassles send me into a tailspin. I find out how much my faithfulness depends on good feelings. And the words of Jesus ring painfully true: "I am the vine, you are the branches. Whoever remains in Me and I in him will bear much fruit, because without Me you can do nothing" (John 15:5).

In reducing me to nothing—or at least, making me feel like nothing—desolation unmasks the secret pride behind my chronic discouragement. It reminds me that the same applause-junkie, trophy-counting perfectionist impulse that gets me into trouble in the rest of life also corrupts my spiritual life. By wavering in resolve or threatening to quit a good work each time I face a fresh bout of desolation, I'm essentially blackmailing God for consolations. I'm demanding the same continual reassurance that three-year-old Joseph demanded of me each time he used the potty for the first few weeks of toilet training. *See how well I did, Mommy? See how I wiped? See how I washed my hands? Clap, Mommy, clap! You forgot to clap! I need a sticker!*

It's cute in a toddler. For about a month. Then the stickers stop because the skill is learned and we have new heights to scale. And because we don't want Mr. Adorable to become Mr. Unbearable.

It's the same with God. He loves me; He's happy to lavish praise on even my meager efforts and He knows how much encouragement I need. Like any good parent, though, He loves me too much to leave me a baby forever. God wants me to grow into a disciple who doesn't need the carrot of consolation to keep her hand to the plow. "When I was a child, I used to talk as a child, think as a child, reason as a child," Paul says. "When I became a man, I put aside childish things" (1 Cor 13:11). Desolation invites me to do the same, to serve the Lord no matter how I feel, and trust that what He told me in the good times still holds true in the bad.

All silver linings aside, most of us would happily swap the cold rain of desolation for the cozy quilt of consolation. But not all consolations are created equal. Which brings us to the third key takeaway from the Ignatian discernment rules: Before we let pleasant feelings and pious inspirations send us sprinting in a new direction for God, we should pause to consider where they came from and where they're leading.

That's rarely what we want to do in the throes of consolation, of course. These intoxicating spiritual highs are a foretaste of heaven, inflaming our hearts with love and joy and strength to do good. We don't want to analyze them. We want to enjoy.

God wants us to enjoy, too. He sends consolations, Ignatius says, "to give true happiness and spiritual joy, and to banish all the sadness and disturbances which are caused by the enemy." Ignatius believed our good feelings and the consolations that produce them can be legitimate ways to discern God's voice. That was his original insight about discernment, after all: that God speaks through our desires and the thoughts and plans that bring us joy.

Yet as Ignatius learned firsthand, the devil can use pleasant thoughts and feelings, too. He knows how to, as Ignatius writes, "suggest holy and pious thoughts that are wholly in conformity with the sanctity of the soul." Then little by little, he uses those holy thoughts for unholy ends, "drawing the soul into his hidden snares and evil designs."

Among those snares are distraction and overcommitment, perennial temptations for perfectionists. We want to give our best to God. Sometimes, though, we get ahead of ourselves in figuring out what that best is. We chase seemingly good ideas without considering their source then wind up depleted, resentful, and robbed of our peace. That's no small victory for Satan, who is happy to begin with minor detours in his quest to lure us off the road to eternal life.

Ignatius advises us to avoid these detours by testing our consolations as Jesus tells us to test prophets: "By their fruits you will know them. . . . A good tree cannot bear bad fruit, nor can a rotten tree bear good fruit" (Matt. 7:16a, 18). No matter how lovely a consolation begins, if it winds up leaving us restless, cranky, weary, dissatisfied, or distracted from the good God already has called us to do, we can bet it's not from Him.

I tasted the rotten fruit of one of these false consolations recently. John was out for the night with friends; I'd had the kids all day and evening and was looking forward to a break the next morning, when I had four hours of writing time reserved for work on this book. I was making good progress on my latest chapter and I wanted an early start to keep the momentum going. I planned to pray a quick rosary, then get right to sleep.

As I climbed into bed and prepared to pray, I found my attention suddenly seized by a new book idea, one that arrived entirely unbidden. The more I pondered it, the more brilliant it seemed. So I pecked some notes about it into my smartphone and settled in to pray.

Then another idea came. This one seemed even better than the first—and more urgent. I turned it over in my mind, analyzing it, basking in it, dreaming of all the good I could do for God if I pulled it off. I tapped a few more notes into my phone, then picked up my rosary again.

No sooner had I done that than another idea arrived. And another. I couldn't decide which I liked better; they all seemed terrific. I usually arrived at my ideas only after months of deliberation and with much trepidation and prayer. On this night, it felt as if someone had turned on a spigot of inspiration and everything that poured out was pure gold.

I sat there for an hour and a half, seized by what felt like one heaven-sent idea after another, adding the occasional note in my phone and following an increasingly grandiose course of thoughts as they led me from one happy fantasy of my literary future to another. I knew it was getting late and I should to get to bed; a little voice inside me warned that all this late-night focus on the next book might not be good for the one I needed to write now. I was relishing my cascade of inspiration too much to shut it off, though. Sleep—and prayer—could wait.

You can guess how this story ends. I didn't say my rosary. I fell asleep two hours past my usual bedtime and awoke too exhausted to do much more than putter on my chapter the next morning. I slogged through the rest of my day, cross with the kids and mad at myself. As for those brilliant book ideas, I couldn't remember most of them by morning. The ones I did remember seemed more half-baked than brilliant.

I had followed the siren song of a false consolation. My nocturnal brainstorming session had all the Ignatian hallmarks of a stinker: It started with thoughts of glorifying God and ended in thoughts of my own glory; it distracted me from prayer and nudged me toward something "less good than the soul had formerly proposed to do," as Ignatius would say; and it rendered me too wiped out to give God my best the next day as a mother and a writer.

There's something else, too, something Ignatius writes about in one of his most intriguing discernment rules: My false consolation came in a burst of excitement that felt almost frenzied. It shook me out of the peaceful contentment I was feeling before it arrived and left me so jazzed and restless that I tossed and turned the rest of the night.

Why does that matter? Because, Ignatius says, in the soul of someone living in union with God—not someone perfect, mind you, but someone "progressing to greater perfection"—consolations from God don't feel like that. The action of God in a soul already striving to please Him "is delicate, gentle, delightful," Ignatius says, like "a drop of water penetrating a sponge" or someone "coming into his own house when the doors are open."

The action of an evil spirit on a God-fearing soul is different. Ignatius describes it as "violent, noisy, and disturbing" like "a drop of water falling upon a stone." Satan has to work harder to break into territory held by God, and Ignatius says the "noise and commotion" we feel during a false consolation—exciting though it may be—are tremors of that unseen spiritual clash.

This is subtle stuff. The more I've paid attention to my consolations, though, the more I've observed the difference Ignatius describes. The consolations that come from God leave me more peaceful, joyful, and free. The ones not of God start off thrilling or exhilarating but tend to spark a certain drivenness in me—a compulsion to do this thing *right now* and not waste *a single minute more* thinking it over lest I miss my opportunity. I still fall prey to them at times, but when I do, I try to follow the advice of Ignatius and "review immediately the whole course of the temptation" to learn from my mistakes.

The final takeaway from the Ignatian discernment method isn't a takeaway at all. It's a prayer.

The Examen, as it's known, is a prayer that Ignatius prayed every day of his post-conversion life—every hour, by some accounts. He required his Jesuits to pray it twice daily, at noon and bedtime. It was the one prayer he never permitted them to skip.

Ignatius saw fidelity to this brief guided reflection as the key to integrating discernment into daily life. The Examen, when prayed daily, helps us learn to distinguish the voice of our Divine Lover from that of the seducer, to sift our spiritual experiences in real time. It's a powerful tool for hearing the whisper of the Holy Spirit over the screeching of the world and our emotions. And for my money, it's the best gift Ignatius left his fellow perfectionists.

Ignatius sketched a bare outline of the Examen in his *Spiritual Exercises*; Jesuits and their fellow travelers have been refining and rewording it ever since. One of my favorite takes is that of Gallagher in his book *The Examen Prayer*. He summarizes the Examen's five essential elements as gratitude (giving thanks to God), petition (asking for the grace to see ourselves as God does), review (considering what's happened since the day started and how we've responded, with an emphasis on discerning the different spirits we've encountered), forgiveness (asking pardon for sins), and renewal (asking God's help with what comes next).

It's a simple sequence, but transformative once you get in the habit—*if* you pray it the right way. The wrong way, at least for

spiritual perfectionists, is to concentrate so intensely on review-
ing every detail of the day, and every real or perceived fault, that
the Examen becomes torturously long, a meticulous exercise in
mental self-flagellation.

If you approach it that way, you'll quit. (I speak from experience.) But if you focus your Examen on gratitude—if you spend
more time looking for the blessings God has lavished on you than
your failures to capitalize on them—you'll look forward to this
brief daily check-in and its joyful surprises. You'll discover hidden sins, yes, but you'll also discover God's grace moving through
people and situations you never noticed before. And you'll start
spotting the devil's maneuvers before they get the better of you.

I've seen it in my own life. My daily Examen has stayed my
hand when I was about to fire off an indignant text based on
what turned out to be a huge misunderstanding; calmed my jit-
ters when I felt too overwhelmed to make an important call that
proved crucial to a professional success; removed my blinders
when I'd spent hours stewing over an injustice done to me before
realizing, just minutes into my Examen, that I was the one who
needed to apologize.

There are days when I collapse into my couch too worn out to
manage anything more than the gratitude step of the Examen. Yet
even that step bears fruit. I find that counting my blessings on a
bad day—even when all I can come up with is the ray of sunshine
peeking through the trees at me or the fact that I didn't melt
down when correcting my toddler for his umpteen meltdowns or
that I have a toddler to correct in the first place—even those
simple observations, when joined to longing for God, can part
the clouds in my soul. And sometimes an Examen that begins as
a chore morphs into a ravishing taste of intimacy with Jesus that

reduces me to tears as I contemplate a gift of His I hadn't even noticed, a gift I would've missed altogether had I not paused to pray my Examen.

Ignatius once described ingratitude as the worst sin, the evil that gives rise to all others, because "it is a failure to recognize the good things, the graces and the gifts received." He saw discernment not only as a way to spot the evil of Satan but as a way to rediscover the goodness of God. Discernment opens our eyes to "the light that shines in the darkness," a light that the darkness has not and never will overcome (John 1:5).

The antidote for my discouragement and distraction isn't only discernment, then. It's gratitude. Gratitude for foggy nights as well as sun-dappled days, gratitude for the Lord's inch-by-inch guidance down those dark roads for which the planner in me would prefer floodlights and GPS.

On those roads, on those nights, Jesus often gives no more direction than what I need to get around the next bend. But He's there. In my desolation and confusion, in my forgetfulness and even my ingratitude—He's there.

That alone is reason to give thanks.

6

A PASSIONATE BALANCE

You will keep him in perfect peace,
whose mind is stayed on You,
because he trusts in You.

(Isa. 26:3–4)

When I was a bobby-socked, freckled fifth-grader at St. Patrick Catholic School in Corpus Christi, Texas, I marched in my first and only All Saints Day parade.

The year was 1985, exactly two decades after the close of the Second Vatican Council, and saint parades had gone the way of altar rails and mantillas in most American parochial schools. But St. Patrick's was an exception and my favorite teacher, Mrs. Garcia, bucked the modernist trend that November. She invited her students to celebrate the feast of All Saints by trading our green-plaid uniforms for the costumes of our favorite holy people.

The boys came dressed as bishops and blood-spattered martyrs. The girls mostly opted for the pretty saints: Elizabeth of Hungary and Margaret of Scotland, who were princesses, and sweet-faced Thérèse of Lisieux, who carried roses.

Me, I chose Joan of Arc.

I arrived at our all-school Mass covered in tin-foil-coated cardboard armor, wearing my hair pulled back into a fake bob and wielding a flimsy-but-fierce-looking tin-foil sword. I did my best to look brave, like Joan. It felt good to trade my reserved, studious persona for the getup of a warrior.

I'm not sure how much I knew about Joan, but I remember liking the fact that she had accomplished something tangible. Liberating France from its military enemies impressed me more at age ten than the amorphous aptitude for prayer and service that characterized most other saints. That this fifteenth-century French visionary and soldier had been burned at the stake only added to her mystique. Bland or boring she was not.

There was no shortage of bland or boring in the other saint stories I heard as a child, and in the mushy theology that characterized much of my Catholic youth. Most of the parishes and parochial schools I attended in the 1980s and 1990s were swimming in smiley faces, felt banners, and clichés of Christian niceness. Well-meaning religious instructors strained to make the faith winsome but too often made it sound like little more than a commitment to obey traffic signals. The saints came off as mild-mannered do-gooders, serving God faithfully for no particular reason and with no particular passion. The ragged, eccentric religious figures and Bible stories that occasionally broke through all that niceness felt like habanero on a soggy burrito: They burned a bit, but at least you knew you were awake.

It wasn't until the end of my college years that I found another female saint whose spunk and accomplishments rivaled Joan's.

Reading the biography of Teresa of Ávila that my father gave me at age twenty-one made me want to do great things for God as Teresa had, to feel the same intensity firing my faith as had fired hers.

What I did not aspire to—at ten or twenty-one—was balance. Balance was for good little girls who didn't outshine their classmates or win anything bigger than a perfect attendance prize. Balance, like moderation, was code for mediocrity. And I wanted no part of mediocrity. I wanted to shine.

As early as my days at St. Patrick's, I took comfort in earning straight As and a lead role in the school play no matter which new school or new state I found myself in. There were plenty of both: A mix of my father's nonprofit work and his wanderlust led my family on half a dozen interstate moves before I turned fifteen, and at least twice as many moves between neighborhoods and schools. My brother coped by excelling at sports and charming the in-crowd. I made my mark by winning spelling bees and writing contests, acing tests and casting calls.

My drive to succeed had its costs. In high school, I missed all but two hours of the only prom I attended because I was performing in a college theater production across town the same night. It was a coup to snag a role as a high school student, so I traded the fanfare of a traditional prom pickup—including the fun of showing off the Rolls-Royce my boyfriend had rented to take me to the big dance—for another credit on my college applications.

In college, I partied as hard as anyone but guarded my near-perfect G.P.A. and résumé fiercely. While my roommates were still snoozing after a raucous night on the town, I'd be trudging across a deserted campus to pound out a paper in my windowless editor's office at the journalism school. I took no breaks, even for lunch. The bagel and swig of water that passed for my breakfast would have to hold me all day, until a combination of hypoglyce-mia and harassing calls from friends lured me out after sunset for another night of revelry.

My reawakening of faith near the end of college tempered my play-hard excesses, but I continued to push myself when it came to work. That my work increasingly focused on defending the faith and Gospel values only intensified my dedication to it.

I researched and wrote my first book, *The New Faithful*, in a series of frenzied bursts over the course of a year, pulling all-nighters in my tiny apartment to finish chapters before rushing back out on the road to cram dozens of interviews into a few days of travel. My time as a White House speechwriter was similarly exhausting. Pop-Tarts from the vending machine were my go-to dinner many nights, and it wasn't unheard of to find me at my desk at 11 p.m. on Sunday taking edits by phone from West Wing higher-ups, then find me there again before sunrise on Monday, fielding the president's own questions or an Oval Office summons.

My decision at age twenty-nine to leave the White House and marry John, who was in the middle of medical school in St. Louis, took all the courage I could muster. I'd never before sacrificed work for a relationship. I sacrificed again two years later, when I opted to stay in St. Louis after John's graduation despite better career opportunities that beckoned elsewhere. My father was in the thick of his long battle with Alzheimer's disease, and I didn't want to leave him.

Still, compulsive achievement remained a temptation. John and I were infertile for the first five years of our marriage and I coped largely by leaning into work. In the days before smart-phones, I met deadlines on vacation by lugging along my laptop or frequenting hotel business centers to access work emails and pound out articles. It felt like a guilty pleasure, and sometimes pure addiction, this habit of trading gorgeous afternoons in the islands or Rockies or Alps for a few stolen hours spent fiddling with words on a screen.

It also felt like an escape. I remember hammering out my weekly op-ed column in my father's hospice room two days before he died, then declining my editor's offer to take the next week off. I didn't know Dad would go so soon—I thought he had another few weeks at least—but I still wince at the memory of myself hunched over a laptop next to my comatose father, trying to meet one more deadline before I gave his impending death my undivided attention.

My attention wasn't always divided. Dad and I spent many memorable times together in his last years, and the lessons he learned in dementia about savoring the present moment were ones I learned alongside him—to a point. But it was only when I became a mother that I realized how much more I had to learn and how unbalanced my perfectionist approach to work was.

At first, I tried to maintain the status quo. I already worked from home, which made the transition from self-employed writer to self-employed-stay-at-home mother easier. I returned to writing my newspaper column three weeks after my twins were born, frantically typing about the travails of working moms while propped on a special nursing pillow that allowed me to breastfeed two babies at once with hands free. I resumed public speaking when the twins turned five months and pretaped new episodes of my TV interview show in strenuous two- and three-day spurts twice yearly after their first birthday. Working nights and weekends, I even managed to write a second book, *My Sisters the Saints*, finishing final edits ten days before the birth of my third child, Clara.

A consummate cuddler with dimpled porcelain cheeks, thick tufts of dark hair, and the sweetest disposition I'd ever seen, Clara proved the perfect partner to join me for occasional speaking trips and TV tapings. She was still nursing every few hours when my memoir debuted in late 2012, so she and the rest of the family came along on my whirlwind East Coast book tour. They joined me again the following March, when I traveled to Rome to anchor the Eternal Word Television Network's live coverage of the 2013 election of Pope Francis. It was the ultimate have-it-all scenario: nursing Clara at dawn and taking a morning run through the streets of the Eternal City before eating breakfast with my family, then dolling up for interviews with Vatican bigwigs in St. Peter's Square in front of a worldwide TV audience.

Alas, what worked for a few breathless, sleepless weeks in Rome couldn't work for the long haul back in the States. I discovered that when we moved to D.C. a few months later for the TV news anchor job that prompted my third big decision to sacrifice work for a relationship—this time, for my relationship with my children.

After leaving my TV job and focusing exclusively on mothering and homeschooling the year after Joseph's birth in 2014, then returning to occasional public speaking and writing in 2015, I began to think a lot about balance.

God had made it clear that He still had work for me to do in the world, and I grew edgy and depressed when I stayed away from it too long. Yet I struggled to combine my old way of working with my new duties to family. Short intervals to write frustrated me; who could create something worthwhile in so little time? Long pauses were sometimes worse. I'd take a weekend away to write but work so intensely, with so few breaks for exercise or prayer or sleep, that I'd return more exhausted than ever, with no desire to do it again anytime soon. Then I'd swing back into turbo-mommy mode, resolving to devote my every free moment to family concerns. Soon I'd be back where I began, bored and burned out from playing an all-mommy-all-the-time role that felt as crazy-making as anything I'd experienced in the White House or the anchor chair.

I had the pieces in place to achieve work-life balance—especially after we moved back to St. Louis in 2016 and John took a job that left him two free mornings a week to homeschool while I wrote. Scheduling hurdles weren't my biggest problem, though. They couldn't explain why I'd found balance so elusive even before I had children, why I still pushed myself so hard even after the deadlines disappeared, or why God gave me these dual passions for work and motherhood that sometimes felt so infuriatingly incompatible. Nor could a saner schedule ease my secret fear that the pursuit of balance and the pursuit of excellence were incompatible.

What I needed was a new approach to understanding and cultivating balance, a genuinely biblical way of holding my competing desires and obligations in tension without sacrificing anything crucial, including my peace of soul. I needed time-tested wisdom about work from someone who had struggled with an intense, perfectionist personality, too; someone who had found a way to make our human limits work for us rather than against us; someone who could teach me how to burn passionately for the work of God without burning out.

re limits to how hard and fast you can push others, just
are limits to how hard and fast you can push yourself. A
oderation in the beginning can yield big dividends in the
d incremental progress beats none at all.

ooled by his failure at Vicovaro, Benedict decided to start
ith his second stab at monastic leadership. He used stones
ero's crumbling palace to build a dozen little monasteries.
used about a dozen men and an abbot hand-picked by
t, whose holy reputation soon led Roman nobles to send
ns to him for an education and protection from the moral
of big-city life.

Subiaco monasteries flourished, a little too well, and
t soon became the target of another attempted poisoning.
prit this time was a jealous local priest. Benedict took it as
move on, so he put an assistant in charge of his monas-
d hit the road with a few other monks around 529. They
seventy–two miles southeast to Monte Cassino, a his-
Christian area that had reverted to paganism after being
ed by Goths and Vandals.

edict believed that God wanted him to reconvert the
Local authorities agreed. So sometime around his fiftieth
, he undertook a forty-day Lenten fast. Then he gath-
monks on the eve of Easter and, hoisting a cross before
harged up the mountain toward the temple where the
ade bloody sacrifices to their gods. In true all-or-nothing
fashion, he demolished their pagan altars, burned down
ve of sacred trees, and began building two churches and
tery in their place.

brazenness cost him. Stories abound about the diabolical
s Benedict endured during construction, not to mention

What I needed, as it turned out, was Saint Benedict and his 1,500-year-old Rule.

Since his death in the sixth century, Benedict of Nursia has been hailed as everything from the founder of Western monasticism and father of modern Europe to the bulwark whose model of Christian community saved civilization during the Dark Ages. His acclaim shows no signs of fading today. Contemporary writers from Kathleen Norris and Joan Chittister to Alasdair MacIntyre and Rod Dreher have all cited Benedict as an inspiration for the renewal of hearts and cultures, a patron saint of balance in a world gone mad with extremism.

Given his reputation for moderation, it's interesting that Benedict began his spiritual life as something of an extremist—even, you might say, a fanatic.

We don't have as many details about that life as we'd like. Saint Gregory the Great's slim, miracle-heavy biography, written fifty years after Benedict's death, is all we have to go on other than the Rule for community living that Benedict left his monks. That Rule is famous for its practical wisdom and allowance for human weakness. Yet most modern biographers say its author was more fiery idealist than easygoing pragmatist, a man possessed of what historian Guy-Marie Oury calls "an insatiable thirst for perfection." Benedict's moderation grew out of experiments with excess that purified, but never expunged, that thirst.

Born around 480 in the hill country of central Italy, Benedict burst into the world as the glory of ancient Rome was flickering out. The city had been sacked three times in the decades before his birth; crime and political corruption were rampant, as were abortion and infanticide. The upper classes were no longer marrying or having babies in large numbers. The lower classes were plagued by hunger and disease. In the Church, the picture wasn't much rosier: more confusion, division, and decay.

The people of Benedict's hometown followed Rome's troubles but were shielded by the seventy mostly mountainous miles that separated them from the city. Although there were nobles in their midst—Benedict's parents among them—Nursians were the antithesis of the effete, conniving Roman patricians of the time. They were tough, physically and morally, known for their rugged independence, austerity, and deep faith.

Benedict was a son of Nursia in every way. So it's no surprise that when his parents sent him to Rome for higher education in his late teens, he was less than impressed by what he saw there. Benedict appreciated the city's splendors but its violence and vice made him fear for his soul and eventually sent him heading for the hills—literally. Taking his family nurse along with him, Benedict fled Rome as a young man and never returned.

After a brief stop in a town thirty miles east of Rome, the runaway scholar parted ways with his nurse and headed for the ruins of what once had been Nero's lakeside pleasure palace in Subiaco. There he holed up in a cave. With the help of an older monk who slipped him food often enough to keep him alive, Benedict communed with God in solitude.

He spent three years that way, praying and persevering alone with God through hunger and cold, doubt and desperation, boredom and temptation. His trials and their remedies were equally severe: Once, when seized by lustful thoughts about a woman he had known in Rome, Benedict stripped off his animal-skin tunic and ran naked into a thornbush to flee the temptation. He had

seen worldly monks in the city and wa[s] [cor]ruption or compromises. Benedict wan[ted] hermits he had admired as a boy, the [Desert] Desert Fathers, took their love of God [...]

The solitary life was Benedict's d[...] plans. Beginning with a priest who p[...] Easter, Benedict began to attract a stea[dy] ing his advice. It wasn't long before a [...] hermits persuaded him to become abb[ot of a mon]astery in the cliffs of nearby Vicovaro.

The Vicovaro monks were a ragtag [...] accustomed to following his own sch[edule in the] privacy of his own cave. Benedict deci[ded ...] to live by a common schedule and con[...] swift and strict, and his attempts to [...] tines of communal life went over like [...] tried to poison him. He returned to h[is cave.]

Benedict's solitude lasted only a [...] mits arrived seeking his direction. Be[nedict felt] calling him to unite these scattered [...] spiritual dangers of seeking holiness [...] of a faith community and the stabili[ty ...] learned from the revolt at Vicovaro, [...] they're humble and charitable when [...] and pursuing their own projects. It's [...] plans that they can see themselves a[nd ...] the virtues they lack.

The revealing nature of commu[nity ...] as well as his monks. A zealous refor[mer ...] of tepidity or time-wasting, Benedic[t ...]

harassment from his predictably peeved neighbors. His preaching and charity to the poor won them over, though, and it wasn't long before Monte Cassino was a flourishing center of evangelization, education, and culture for a region desperately in need of all three.

Benedict lived nearly two more decades in Monte Cassino, until his death in 547 at age sixty-seven. It was there in Monte Cassino that he finally realized his vision of a monastic life that mingled lofty worship of God with nitty-gritty service to neighbor, a life that honored our dual callings to *ora et labora*, as the Benedictine motto goes: pray and work. And it was in the give-and-take of this balanced, communal life that, in the words of biographer Ildephonsus Herwegen, "what seemed hard and perhaps iron in the will of Benedict was softened, while the violent and hasty elements in him were restrained." The result was a man utterly at peace even as he retained his consuming zeal for God's work. Benedict's spirit became, Herwegen says, a blend "of strength and tenderness, of law and liberty, of nature and grace, of objective rule and individual life . . ."

Benedict did more than reach spiritual maturity at Monte Cassino. He also wrote the Rule there that would become a foundational document of Western civilization, a synthesis of Scripture, earlier monastic rules, and Benedict's hard-won wisdom that Herwegen calls "a compendium of his own life." The Rule offers us a glimpse of the daily habits and practices that softened the saint's rough edges and those of his monks. And in the Rule, we find a blueprint for biblical balance aimed squarely at strivers like Benedict—and us.

My biggest surprise when I first read the Rule of Benedict was how clear, how concrete, how *ordinary* it is. It's a document writ-

ten nearly a thousand years before the invention of the print-
ing press, by a man who spent his formative years in a cave, for
monks scrapping their livelihood out of a rocky cliff. Yet like the
Bible on which it is based, the Rule speaks vividly and practically
to issues I'm facing today. With a little adaptation, it can serve
equally well as a guide to life in a family or parish or close-knit
workplace as it can to life in a monastery.

That's largely because of the author's active, multifaceted life.
Benedict was a layperson writing for laypeople, a man who knew
well our experience of wearing many hats and juggling many
tasks. He and his monks spent their days teaching children, hosting guests, tending the sick, feeding the hungry, copying manu-
scripts, practicing trades, pricing goods, and managing coworkers.
As Anglican author and mother of four Esther de Waal writes,
Benedict's Rule describes life "as most of us experience it: a cease-
less round of daily duties, cooking and then serving and then
washing up; constant attention to the needs and claims of others,
and all this probably in addition to the particular job for which we
have been professionally trained."

Benedict saw those daily duties as the stuff of our sanctification. For Benedict, holiness consists in fidelity to God's will amid
the competing demands on our time and the mundane tasks of
everyday life. While other saints tutor us on the three stages of
spiritual progress or the five proofs for God's existence, Benedict
tells us the best way to clean the kitchen after supper or greet
strangers at the door. His specificity can be off-putting at times;
do I really need to know how a monk should chant Psalm 66 at
Lauds or how many pounds of bread he should eat a day? But
those details underscore the Rule's deeper message: that how we
do things matters as much as or more than what we do. And the

very tasks we regard as trivial time-wasters may be the ones keeping our egos in check and our lives in balance.

Benedict's focus on fidelity in the ordinary goes a long way toward explaining the Rule's view of work. Like the Desert Fathers before him, Benedict saw great spiritual value in work. By forcing us to meet objective standards, demanding our full attention, and reconnecting us to the world outside ourselves, work serves as a powerful antidote against daydreaming, melancholy, self-absorption, and sluggishness. Work, when approached the right way, leads us to deeper and more fruitful prayer. It can even become a prayer in itself.

So what's the right approach to work? Benedict suggests that it begins with an acknowledgment that our work, like everything good in our lives, belongs to God before it belongs to us. Our talents, our ideas, our opportunities—all are gifts of grace, Benedict believed. While the Lord gives us the freedom to use them in His service or not, the fruitfulness of our efforts ultimately depends on Him, not us.

This reliance on grace—in work, and in all of life—is a running theme in the Rule. Benedict was born only sixty years after the death of Pelagius, the notorious spiritual perfectionist who denied original sin and said we could get to heaven without God's help. Pelagius was excommunicated and his errors were attacked or condemned by three separate church councils. But a watered-down form of his heresy, Semi-Pelagianism, was still enough of a threat in Benedict's day that Benedict felt compelled to repeatedly reaffirm the necessity of grace in his Rule.

From its Prologue, where Benedict urges us to "beg God to supply by the help of His grace that which by nature is lacking to us," to its last chapter, where he characterizes all he has discussed as "only the beginning of perfection," the loftier heights of which—like its first steps—are reached only "with the help of God's providence," Benedict stresses that we can't complete or even start our journey to holiness without grace. We still need to cooperate with grace; as we pursue "the perfect love that casts out all fear," Benedict says, we must "run [to God's kingdom] by doing good deeds." But it is grace that makes those deeds possible and fruitful.

Part of relying on grace is admitting that we can't do everything we want to do when we want to do it. That's asking a lot of an achievement addict, and Benedict knew as well as anyone the sense of urgency that can leave perfectionists antsy and panicked at the passage of time. His own sense of urgency pulses from the third paragraph of his Rule, where he quotes Jesus—"Walk while you have the light, so that darkness may not overcome you" (John 12:35)—but with a twist. "Run while you have the light," Benedict urges, after assuring us, "My words are meant for you, whoever you are . . . let us arise without delay, the Scriptures stirring us . . ."

We must be ready to run, Benedict believes, yet we must also be ready to acknowledge the limits on how far we can go any given day. That's where habits and routines come in. Benedict devoted much of his Rule to outlining schedules that ensured his monks got enough time each day to pray, work, eat, rest, read, and study Scripture. Benedict saw our daily routines as a concrete expression of our priorities, and a reliable way to keep first things first. It's one thing to say we love God. It's another to drop what we're doing seven or eight times a day for communal prayer, as monks who follow Benedict's Rule did, and still do.

Benedict knew how hard it can be to stop what you're doing to get to chapel or dinner or bed on time. Alongside his suggested schedules, he includes tips for handling those who blow them—including the workaholics who always want to finish one more thing at quitting time. His punishments can be harsh: Latecomers to night prayer have to stand in the lowest place in church and do public penance; chronic dawdlers to dinner have to eat alone and forgo wine. Ever the realist, though, Benedict advises that the first psalm of night prayer be said slowly to give stragglers a chance to slide in before being counted tardy.

The Rule's focus on prompt arrivals is less about punctuality than obedience—obedience to what God is asking of us in the present moment. Benedict understood the importance of pursuing excellence and completing tasks with care; he reminds us that since God sees everything we do, we should do everything "that God may be glorified." But there's a fine line between work that glorifies God and work that merely glorifies ourselves. Benedict saw our willingness to drop our work when a more pressing need arises as a good indicator of whether or not we've crossed that line.

He also saw it as a good indicator of our diligence. While we tend to consider hard-working the guy who skips family dinners and Sunday church to put in more time at the office, Benedict would consider him lazy. Anyone who can't shut up and sit still long enough to pray, read, and study God's Word is "slothful," Benedict says, and he should do extra manual labor to curb his addiction to "idleness."

That work can easily slide from God-centered mission to self-centered escape is a truth Benedict hammers home in his chapter on the abbey's artisans. The wares of these skilled craftsmen often brought in the bulk of the monastery's income, but Benedict didn't see that as an excuse for vanity or workaholism. Let them "practice their crafts with humility . . ." he writes. "But if anyone becomes proud of his skill and the profit he brings the community, he should be taken from his craft and work at ordinary labor." Better to lose your trade and waste your talent than forfeit your soul.

Does all this emphasis on humility and break-taking mean that the Rule is anti-achievement? One look at the history books answers that question. At a time when the rest of the Western world was mired in chaos and barbarism, Benedictine monks and nuns were building cathedrals and hospitals, cultivating farmland, transcribing books, and educating generations of artists, scholars, and saints. Many still do that work today.

Yet they do so following a Rule that defines success very differently than does our world. A successful life, in the Benedictine view, is not one dominated by niche achievement pursued through a narrow focus on one area of specialization. Nor is it something you can quantify: dollars earned, honors won, people served.

For Benedict and his followers, a successful life is one that leads to union with God. It's a whole-life project that demands our complete commitment and engages every aspect of our personality and identity. Work can be a means of pursuing it, but eternity is its end. And while external accomplishments can signal our progress toward that end, our willingness to accept limits on those achievements for love of God is often a better marker.

I first encountered the Benedictine emphasis on accepting limits as a sophomore in high school. That's when my father left his job as director of family life programs for the Catholic diocese of Columbus, Ohio, to become director of a Benedictine retreat center in Colorado Springs.

It was a huge move. One week, I was riding my ten-speed through the humid flatlands of central Ohio. The next, I was gaping slack-jawed at the grandeur of Pikes Peak, my cracked lips and suddenly-straight hair reminding me that I was six thousand feet above sea level and twelve hundred miles from my nearest friend.

Seasoned as I was at moving, it still wasn't easy to break into a tiny private high school where many of my sixty classmates had been besties since kindergarten. Nor was it easy to navigate the first month of life out West without my mother, who was once again hanging behind to wrap up work in our old hometown before heading to the new.

The mountains helped. I'd lived in pretty places before—on a lake in Florida, a block from the bay in Texas, on the edge of a stunning, shaded ravine in Ohio—but nothing prepared me for the daily thrill of living beside the Rockies. I had no idea that mountains had so many ways of being beautiful. They could be sparkling and clear, moody and forbidding, silken and mystical, all in the same day. And I could see it all from my bedroom window in our little neon-green house, which sat high atop the Austin Bluffs overlooking the Front Range.

The home was part of Dad's compensation package from the Benedictine sisters, who made up for a lackluster salary by offering us free housing on the same campus as their own cluster of homes. Another perk was free food: Our family was invited to join them every night for dinner in their cafeteria.

For a high school student bent on fitting in and looking cool, it was the setup from hell. Luckily, my cooler older brother was already off to college and I didn't have enough style to cramp.

At least, not until I started dating and had to explain who those gaggles of old ladies were who were always peeking out of the neighboring houses to wave at me or cluck at me not to take the hills too fast or check their watches when I came home too late.

I didn't know much about Benedictine spirituality then, and I was too consumed by my own high school dramas to learn. Still, I absorbed a few lessons by osmosis. Most came via Sister Diane.

A sprightly, old-school Scripture scholar who loved the Pauline epistles and Rocky Mountains with equal vigor, Sister Diane organized hikes every Saturday morning for herself and whoever else in the community wanted to join her. She left from her house at 7 a.m. sharp. If you wanted to go, you had to arrive on time, wearing decent shoes and plenty of layers, with a snack, water bottle, and packed lunch in hand.

I don't recall what convinced me to get up at dawn on that first Saturday morning and hop into a rusty, sputtering hatchback with a fifty-something nun I barely knew. Probably Dad prodded me, and I hadn't yet made enough friends to have better plans.

As Sister Diane adjusted the barrette in her gray bob and put a scuffed hiking boot to the pedal, I wasn't sure what to expect. My family was big on organized sports but our hikes always had been rare, spur-of-the-moment affairs. Dad would be driving us somewhere—maybe to gawk at scenery on our way to dinner, maybe to vacation a few days at the home of some old friend who had not yet been informed that our family of four was coming to stay—and he'd spot a trail off the side of the road. He'd swerve over and pop out of the car, grinning and ready to take the summit. We'd file out and follow for a while, until someone got thirsty (we never brought water) or cold (we didn't do layers) or realized that flip-flops weren't proper footwear for scaling rocks. Maybe we'd hit an unexpected storm (we rarely checked weather) or get lost (Dad wasn't big on maps). There would be a few nail-biting moments when we weren't sure we'd make it back. Eventually, though, we always did. Then we'd pile back into the car and Dad would scout out a good steak place where we could refuel and laugh over our latest brush with disaster.

Hiking with Sister Diane was different. Everything was planned, from which trail we were taking to which spot on the trail we'd stop for a snack and what time we'd eat lunch. She knew the mountains well enough to spot early signs of foul weather and always timed outings so we were on the descent before the afternoon thunderstorms hit.

At first, I chafed against all that predictability. What's the fun of a hike if you know exactly where you're going and when you'll return? Who needs to rest and snack two hours into a climb when you could reach the top faster if you pushed through without stopping?

Something about the rhythm of those Saturdays with Sister Diane appealed to me, though. I found myself making time for hikes with her even after I had other offers. It felt good to work my body hard, to breath the thin air at the summit of a challenging trail, to look out over miles upon miles of evergreens and purple peaks and realize how little, in the grand scheme, all of my troubles were—how little I was. It also felt good to care for myself along the way, to wear what I needed and drink what I needed and eat what I needed and rest when I needed. It felt as if life were manageable, peaceful, balanced.

The passion for hiking that Sister Diane instilled in me went dormant during my college years in Wisconsin but returned a decade later when I met John. Exploring the limestone bluffs and rolling hills of central Missouri became our favorite pastime together, and John proposed to me during one of our Ozark hikes. Now we hike with our children whenever we can. We always remember to check the forecast, pack enough water and snacks, and choose trails that won't stretch our little climbers past their limits.

The notion of limits as something to accept and work within, rather than to ignore or rage against, is distinctly Benedictine. It's also profoundly countercultural.

Everywhere we turn in our culture, and sometimes even in the Church, we are urged to challenge our limits. Don't accept any reality short of doing it all, having it all, being all you want to be, we are told. If you can believe it, you can achieve it.

There's something liberating about admitting that's a lie.

We are finite creatures. We have limited power, partial knowledge, fixed conditions under which we operate. That's what it means to be human. It's a reality that even Jesus accepted, when He became like us in all things but sin (Heb. 4:15). We're naturally wowed by the miracles that manifested Christ's divinity. But equally astounding was His willingness to share our humanity: to suffer the same hunger and thirst, temptation and time constraints as we do; to live within the confines of a particular body, a particular time and place and family.

Jesus accepted the reality of human limits out of love for us and obedience to His Father. It only makes sense, then, for us to do the same.

There are times when God explodes our limits, of course. Scripture says "nothing will be impossible for God" (Luke 1:37) and "I can do all things through Christ who strengthens me"

(Phil. 4:13). Yet Scripture also reminds us that not everything we aim to achieve, not every victory we want over our limits, is God's will. As Paul explained, when lamenting the "thorn in the flesh" he never could shake,

> *Three times I begged the Lord about this, that it might leave me, but He said to me, 'My grace is sufficient for you, for power is made perfect in weakness.' . . . Therefore, I am content with weaknesses, insults, hardships, persecutions, and constraints, for the sake of Christ; for when I am weak, then I am strong (2 Cor. 12:8–10).*

I've read that passage many times, but it was only after studying the Rule that I noticed the significance of Paul's word choice in its last sentence. In the face of all those weaknesses and setbacks, Paul doesn't say that he is working to rise above them or even gritting his teeth and bearing with them. He says that he's content.

That's a challenging concept. To be content with constraints is much tougher, at least for this perfectionist, than to try to overcome or escape them. With an escape attempt, at least I'm doing something. I might be wasting my time, pursuing a phantom goal that's distracting me from the real one God has set before me. But I'm setting the agenda. I'm calling the shots.

Contentment is harder. It requires me to accept reality as I find it in this moment—the tasks I have to do today, the people I have to serve this hour, the flaws in myself and my life that I can't fix right now. Contentment means leaving the big picture to God while I muddle through the day-to-day. And I hate muddling.

The reasons I find contentment so difficult are the very reasons I need to practice it. Sometimes God works through the hasty and heroic fixes I favor. More often, though, He works slow-and-steady transformations in the midst of my daily grind. What He asks of me in that process is obedience: obedience to the demands of my life as it is, not as I wish it were.

That obedience can hurt. When I can't meet my goals because I'm too busy meeting everyone else's needs; when my schedule is blown by the flare-up of a chronic problem that I can't solve, only manage; when respecting my body's need for sleep or God's Sabbath command to rest means leaving work undone that desperately needs doing—obedience feels like an imposition, an affront to my autonomy.

Yet the Rule says obedience is my ticket to freedom, by way of humility. A humble person, Benedict says, "does not bother to please himself, but follows the injunction of the Lord: 'I came not to do My own will, but the will of Him who sent Me'" (John 6:38). The humble surrender of my will is a struggle, but even attempting it makes me feel freer.

When I try to obediently accept some unavoidable constraint as a manifestation of God's will, the shift in my attitude is palpable. I feel the tension easing out of my back and neck as I shake off the weight of what-must-get-done and breathe in the peace of just-do-what-I-can. I find myself working with greater joy and abandon, knowing that if I'm no longer setting the agenda then I'm no longer on the hook for the outcome. And I feel myself listening more for the inspirations of the Holy Spirit, because I'm no longer terrified they'll scuttle my plans.

Accepting my limits requires me to trust God more, which in turn fosters more trust in God. It's a virtuous cycle. When I let go of things I can't do, or can't do as quickly or perfectly as I'd planned, I discover that God has other ways of getting His work done. Sometimes someone else steps in and does what I thought only I could do. Sometimes the urgent task that tempts me to turn my world upside down turns out to be optional and I realize after letting it go that it didn't matter much anyway. Sometimes things turn out less than ideal and I discover that settling for an imperfect outcome with my peace intact is an achievement in itself.

Workaholism, like perfectionism, enthrones me at the center of my life: my goals, my timelines, my ego. It is inherently solitary and self-centered. But accepting my limits—both by recognizing God's will in the needs of loved ones that scramble my schedule and by admitting I can't always meet those needs as well as I'd like—draws me out of myself. I remember my weakness and need, my role as part of a larger whole. I discover that God's got this even if I don't; that I'm irreplaceable but not indispensable.

I discover something else, too: If the Lord doesn't need me to do His work, if my participation in building His kingdom is a privilege He confers rather than a payment He demands, then my worth no longer depends on my achievements. I no longer need to prove myself by what I do. And my attempts to do so by ignoring my limits start to seem downright silly.

The full extent of their silliness only dawned on me recently, on an otherwise forgettable Wednesday afternoon last fall.

I had just arrived home after writing all morning at the library. I was breathless—I'm almost always breathless when returning from writing, because I get too engrossed in what I'm doing to watch the clock—and I had barely made it back in time to take over with the kids so John could get to work. I was still clutching my laptop as I gave him a quick good-bye kiss, then called my children to come in from the backyard for lunch.

Three hungry kids tumbled inside, ready to eat. But my oldest son, eight-year-old John Patrick, lagged behind. He was in the middle of a construction project and didn't appreciate the interruption.

John Patrick loves to build, and he's good at it. He has a great heart, too: After hearing stories of so many saints who served the poor, he decided last year to create a house for the homeless behind our own. His father gave him some lumber scraps and he's been hard at work ever since. It's a great project for a little guy with loads of imagination and a knack for organization.

But John Patrick struggles to tear himself away. I've had to remind him more than once about the importance of cheerful, prompt obedience even when you're doing something that feels more important than feeding your body or heeding your mommy.

That afternoon, as he came stomping into the kitchen and I drew a breath to lecture him, what came out instead was a laugh. Here I was, frantic from having abandoned my writing mid-sentence and still mulling the best way to finish the troublesome paragraph that felt far more compelling in that moment than lunch with my four squawking children. I was smiling at them through gritted teeth, but what I really wanted to do was get back to my book.

Like mother, like son.

The irony—of me winding up to rebuke my child for the same meager, grudging obedience that I was giving to God—was too rich to resist. So I laid my laptop on the kitchen counter and plopped on the floor.

"I know exactly how you feel, John Pat," I called up to him, as I got down on all fours and pressed my left cheek to the linoleum.

My son's grumpy face turned quizzical as I began to beat my fists and feet on the ground.

"I don't want lunch," I wailed. "I want to write!"

The other kids scurried over to watch. John Patrick stood above me, his gaping mouth slowly curving into a smile.

"Mommy's throwing a tantrum!"

"Ahh!" I hollered, over the delighted shrieks of my children. "It's not fair. It's not FAIR!"

John Pat was convulsed with giggles now, struggling for air as he repeated my favorite scolds back to me.

"It's time to eat, Mommy. You can finish later. You can't work all day. NO TANTRUMS!"

"Noooo!"

"Yes, Mommy! You have to get up."

"No!"

"Yes!"

"No!"

"Yes!"

"OK, fine."

With a wink, I was back on my feet. We were both laughing. It felt good to admit that accepting our limits is hard—and that denying them always looks a little ridiculous.

I'd like to say that was the last time I was ever tempted to pout or push against my limits. Of course, it wasn't. Accepting the reality of my finite time and energy is an ongoing struggle, and I suspect it will be until I die.

The good news is that I'm getting better.

The Rule has taught me to step outside my old workaholic habits and observe myself when I feel that familiar tug of compulsion. My first instinct when I run out of work time is still frustration many days, but now it's almost always followed by the realization that God is inviting me to an act of humble, cheerful obedience. I don't always make it, but that image of my kitchen-floor tantrum helps me remember that it's a better bet than the alternative.

The Rule also has changed how I spend my work time. Even when I'm crashing on deadline and holed up in a retreat house for a long-awaited writing weekend, I've learned that I still need to take regular breaks to eat, pray, run, rest, and even play. Last month, I slipped out for a date night in the middle of my writing weekend because it was the only time John and I could get a sitter. This month, I knocked off early to hit the St. Patrick's Day parade with my little Irish lasses and lads. Some things are just too much fun to miss.

The Rule has persuaded me that since God cares about my whole self—body, mind, and spirit—I need to do the same. That means watching for signs of fatigue, hunger, and burnout in myself, just as I do in my kids. It also means refusing to feel angst over what's undone when my work time is up and trusting that God will help me pick up where I left off another day.

The more I've worked on respecting my limits, the more I've noticed something: Human creativity flourishes amid constraints. Maybe it's because we're creatures instead of the Creator; maybe it's because necessity is the mother of invention. All I know is that I don't suffer from writer's block nearly as often as I did before I had kids. Back then, I could waste an entire day wondering what to write. Now, if I have two hours to write, I spend them writing.

I've observed something similar with interruptions. More times than I can count, I've interrupted my writing to care for children or parents or myself only to return to it the next day with an entirely new—and better—perspective. That good night's sleep I didn't want to settle down for, that visit to the adoration chapel for which I reluctantly traded my last hour of work time, that family outing or visit to my mom that I was tempted to skip so I could write a little longer: not only were they the right thing to do, but they saved me from wasting hours heading in the wrong direction with a challenging chapter or furnished me with fresh inspiration to express an insight I couldn't quite articulate the day before. The breaks I don't want to take often are the ones I need most.

The same goes for breaks from mothering; just ask my husband. John is the first one to push me out the door on my writing days, when I'm running low on inspiration and wondering if a better mother would stay home to clean closets or research summer camps. He prods me through writing rough patches with early-morning emails of encouragement and Scripture. When I'm despairing of juggling work and motherhood and chewing over my latest encounter with naysayers—both the anti-work types who think the only good mommy is a housebound martyr, and the anti-kid types who seem to think a woman's brain leaves her body with the placenta of her fourth child—John reminds me that their opinions don't count. God's does. And God has called me to write.

John knows that I'm a happier wife and mother when I'm writing. He also believes that our children need to see that Mommy has other interests and talents besides caring for them. They don't have to be paid pursuits, but they do have to be my own. Just as I need to take breaks from my work to nourish my family, so I need to take breaks from my family to care for myself. And for me, self-care includes stretching my intellectual and artistic muscles, honing my professional skills, and seeing what good I can do in the world with the gifts I've been given.

None of which is to say that I don't feel occasional twinges of sadness at trade-offs I've made or envy toward those who seem to have made fewer trade-offs than me. But I've come to see that the gifts and limits of my life go hand in hand and I can't embrace one without the other. Nor can I "have it all"—no woman can, whether she works outside the home or not—because all is God's domain, not ours.

My all will come in heaven. What I can have here is balance, the Benedictine balance that de Waal describes as "no easy middle way . . . no recipe for mediocrity." It is, rather, "the holding together in one center of ultimate values," the continual, faith-filled search for an equilibrium point between the various duties and passions of my life.

It would be simpler to be all mommy or all writer, all wife or all daughter, all action or all contemplation. But Benedict has taught me that my faith, like my creativity, is invigorated by the interplay between the diverse callings of my life, by the fact that God has not called me to one role or job but to many. Some of my callings matter more than others; marriage is the primary context God has chosen to sanctify me. But all have value. And the very tension that sometimes feels as if it will pull me apart is actually a healing force, one that keeps me leaning on Jesus as I find my footing in a full, demanding, and ever-changing life.

7

PILGRIMS AND STRANGERS

Therefore, since we are surrounded by so great a cloud of witnesses,
let us rid ourselves of every burden and sin that clings to us
and persevere in running the race . . .
keeping our eyes fixed on Jesus, the leader and perfecter of faith.
For the sake of the joy that lay before Him
He endured the cross, despising its shame,
and has taken His seat at the right of the throne of God.

(Heb. 12:1–2)

I'd been tired all morning, groggy from the humid July air and a
night of spotty sleep. But as soon as I turned our minivan into
my old subdivision, I felt eerily alert. Although I hadn't seen this
street in decades, I found myself instinctively watching for my
best friend Amy darting by on her banana-seat bike, my escaped
calico kittens scurrying through the roadside grasses, and our
well-heeled-but-wacky neighbor lady arguing with herself at full
volume as she strolled past with her bewildered pup in tow.

This neighborhood had always been colorful, teeming with crazy characters and flora and fauna I'd seen only in northern Florida. Of all the homes I'd lived in as a child—including the three I knew in Tallahassee—this was the one I'd loved best.

We had found it just after my father discerned a call to leave the higher pay and prestige of his job at a secular nonprofit to work for the Church. Dad didn't make the switch lightly; he prayed and talked with my mother long hours over the decision. He knew that working for the Catholic Church as a layperson can be a ticket to financial insecurity, especially for a man in his fifties with a wife in graduate school and two children in private schools. But Dad sensed the Lord asking him to trust, so he did. As if to confirm his choice, he discovered after signing on with the Diocese of Tallahassee that a church benefactor was willing to rent out her lake house at a reduced rate to help the new diocesan Director of Family Life make the transition.

Her home was a brick ranch, not the fanciest in this swanky community, but plenty fancy for us. It boasted five bedrooms, three acres on the water, an in-ground pool, and too many azalea and rose bushes to count. The three years we lived here were the stuff of childhood dreams. We hosted pool parties, chased turtles and snakes, spotted alligators on our shoreline, fed horses that lived at the end of the lane, and swam, fished, and canoed to our heart's content. We didn't own a speedboat like most of our neighbors but we caught plenty of rides in them all the same. We even started a brushfire that required half the neighborhood to put out. (Dad thought burning leaves would be more efficient than bagging them; turns out that's not true on a windy day.) The dramas and disasters were almost as much fun as the parties, and in my memory, our time here was just one long sun-drenched summer day.

I had waxed nostalgic about this neighborhood, and this house, for years. So when I finally found myself close enough to visit in person, I asked John to let me drive. I wanted to give the kids and him a proper tour of my idyllic childhood home.

As we pulled up to the house, though, I felt bewildered. The address was correct but I didn't recognize the forlorn digs before me.

There was a for-sale sign lying facedown in the overgrown front yard, which was strewn with wood chips and patches of dirt. The palm trees and bushes that once neatly framed the home's entrance now crowded across its windows and steps, with fronds more dead than alive. The smart blue shutters I remembered were gone; the pool once rimmed with roses was colonized by weeds so tall and tangled that I couldn't open its gate. The gorgeous Spanish-moss-covered oak tree featured in dozens of my favorite childhood photos was now misshapen by what looked to be a botched trim job.

As for the back patio with the breathtaking lake view where we celebrated my First Communion and Mom's graduate school commencement and countless birthday parties, it was so riddled with rubbish, bugs, and broken tiles that I couldn't let my children play on it. When I tiptoed across the debris and cupped my hands to peer in the kitchen window, I spotted the same vinyl flooring that I'd raced my toy cars on as a second-grader thirty-five years ago. It looked as if that was the last time someone had mopped it, too.

"This place looked better when I was a kid," I assured my husband, suddenly regretting how much I'd bragged it up. "You should've seen it then. It was really beautiful."

John and the kids were good sports. They tried to imagine the glories I described. Maryrose said the house just needed some love, and she and fixer-upper John Patrick spent a few impassioned moments trying to convince us to buy and restore it. Clara skipped along raving about the bugs she was spotting in the overgrown grass as we made our way down to the lake that seemed smaller than I remembered.

It was starting to rain as we climbed back up to the street and began wandering the neighborhood. I saw no sign of anyone I recognized. The horses were gone; the cutting-edge 1980s home styles looked dated; the lakeside tennis courts seemed sad and neglected. The kids tried to make some fun of the rusty swings and spring riders they found on the neighborhood playground, but the drizzle soon turned to a downpour and sent us dashing for the car.

As I handed the keys back to John and sank into the passenger seat, I could almost hear Dad repeating his favorite Latin phrase to me.

"*Sic transit Gloria mundi*," he'd say, his Irish eyes twinkling. "Thus passes the glory of the world."

That soggy jog down memory lane was the most startling of my attempts to go home again, but it wasn't the only one that has ended in disappointment. Over the years, I've returned to many of my childhood houses and schools and parishes. I'm always struck by how much smaller they seem, how foreign they feel, and how few people in them remember that I even existed. I usually leave feeling displaced but oddly grateful for a concrete reminder that "we have here no lasting city, but seek the one that is to come" (Heb. 13:14).

The contingent nature of any earthly home is a lived reality for children who grow up as nomadic as I did. But it's a truth intended for everyone. Scripture overflows with warnings that the homes, riches, and reputations we prize aren't nearly as enduring or important as we think.

The theme first surfaces in Genesis, where we find those words still used in Ash Wednesday liturgies: "You are dust, and to dust you shall return" (Gen. 3:19). The psalmist concurs: "Every man is but a breath," he says, and his days are "like the grass" or a "shadow" that "pass quickly and are gone" (Pss. 39:6, 103:15, 144:4, 90:10). Ecclesiastes devotes a dozen chapters to unpacking its jarring opening proclamation that "all things are vanity" (Eccles. 1:2), while the first book of Chronicles concludes with a reminder that "we are strangers and travelers, like all our ancestors" (1 Chron. 29:15).

In the New Testament, James tells us it's foolish to spend our lives making plans, making money, and making a name for ourselves. "You have no idea what your life will be like tomorrow. You are a puff of smoke that appears briefly and then disappears" (James 4:14). Rather than chase riches and reputation, Jesus says, we should "store up treasures in heaven, where neither moth nor decay destroys, nor thieves break in and steal" (Matt. 6:20).

He's right; we should. We know we should.

But if you're like me, you struggle to remember that in the midst of the everyday. You wrap up your morning prayers with good intentions, fully planning to put Jesus and His priorities first. Then the world's demands start pressing in. *Go here, do this, buy that.* Eternal perspective takes a backseat to the need for approval, efficiency, control. You scramble to compete and keep up. Those heavenly treasures begin to fade, suddenly feeling too illusory and insubstantial to interrupt a routine relentlessly driven by the here and now.

The tendency to focus more on stuff, status, and social expectations than the things of God is not unique to perfectionists. Yet perfectionism can magnify it. The same forces and beliefs that drive us to serve a distorted image of God can also make us slaves of human respect. We find ourselves heeding the vox populi more than the Voice of God, worrying more about how we look to others than who we are to Him. We slip into what psychologists call socially prescribed perfectionism, the kind driven by external pressures we feel to be flawless.

It may seem that socially prescribed perfectionism, with its outward focus, is utterly distinct from inward-looking spiritual perfectionism. In fact, the two often go hand in hand. The idol served by a people-pleasing social perfectionist makes surprisingly similar demands to the one served by a shame-ridden spiritual perfectionist. Both drive us to maintain appearances, compare ourselves to others, and prize conformity over freedom and joy.

Where God is concerned, we perfectionists can console ourselves with the promise that "the Lord is gracious and merciful, slow to anger and abounding in mercy" (Ps. 145:8). We can remember all we've learned about who God is and what His grace can do and how much more He values our loving surrender than our self-reliance and willpower.

But what about other people? Just because we're ready to let go of unredeemed standards of perfection and impossible expectations for ourselves doesn't mean that our loved ones, colleagues, and culture are ready to follow suit. Recovery from spiritual perfectionism necessarily entails recovery from social perfectionism, a willingness to embrace Christ's way of perfection even at the cost of ridicule and loss of influence, friends, comfort, and wealth.

That's a scary prospect for anyone, but especially for perfectionists accustomed to winning in the world's eyes. It's one thing to jump off the perfectionist crazy train when others are cheering your courage. It's another to take the leap when everyone around you is shrieking in disapproval, reminding you that it's a long way down and only a fool would try it and *who are you to get out of your seat when the rest of us are buckled in and enjoying the ride?*

Bombarded by those voices, we can find ourselves relapsing endlessly into perfectionist bad habits. We know that the shriekers don't speak for God, that we are aiming for "a better homeland, a heavenly one" (Heb. 11:16). Yet we also know that even if we no longer buy the world's version of perfection, we still must live, work, and worship with people who do.

So how do we live in this perfectionist world but not of it? How do we embrace our identity as "strangers and pilgrims on earth" (Heb. 11:13) when the perks of social conformity seem so much more tangible? And if slipping the bonds of spiritual perfectionism is a long process that unfolds only alongside a similar release from social perfectionism, what are the habits and attitudes we most need to surrender to trade preoccupation with the world's standards for single-minded focus on God's?

At first glance, Francis of Assisi may seem an unlikely saint to help us answer those questions. He was a nonconformist, no doubt: A thirteenth-century playboy-turned-preacher, Francis roamed the Italian countryside shoeless and penniless, sleeping in the open air and singing God's praises to anyone who would listen, animal and human alike. His love for creation and intentional embrace of poverty made him the patron of ecologists, peaceniks, and free spirits of every stripe, not to mention the crowning figure on countless birdbaths and creation-care devotionals. For all his appeal, though, it's hard to imagine Francis sympathizing with our temptations to social perfectionism. Wouldn't this master of self-denial scoff at our modern luxuries, roll his eyes at our concern for appearances, and tell us to drop all that worldliness and just get on with doing God's will already?

The mature Francis might. But the younger one could relate to our struggles. Francis spent more than two decades living in thrall to the same social pressures and temptations to turn back that dog us, pressures that left him teetering on the edge of respectability for a full five years before he finally embraced God's radical call on his life.

That life inspired millions, spurring churchwide renewal in a spiritually moribund period of the Middle Ages, spawning three worldwide religious communities, and awakening generations of lukewarm Christians to the countercultural adventure of Gospel living. It made Francis one of the most beloved saints in history, an evangelist and mystic whose popularity transcends denominations and whose imitation of Jesus earned him the nickname "Mirror of Perfection" because he was said to have lived the most Christlike life since Christ Himself.

That was Francis 2.0: sage, single-minded, and sold out to God. Francis 1.0 was a different story.

He wasn't a bad guy. For the first half of his life, Francis loved the Lord, at least somewhat, and gave generously to the poor. He loved his family and friends. He also loved parties, flashy clothes, and practical jokes. Any given night, this carefree son of a wealthy cloth merchant could be found leading a band of buddies up and down the hilly streets of Assisi, bellowing French love songs, buying the drinks, and acting the clown. Francis was an irrepressibly cheerful mischief-maker, his city's favorite son. Even the sleep-deprived old folks who hollered down from their windows to shush him up couldn't help but smile at his antics.

What made Francis beloved also made his conversion difficult. He wasn't wallowing in the gutter when grace came knocking. He was on top of his game: rich, dapper, popular. It took more than one spiritual wake-up call or test to wean Francis from the good life and his good name, to transform Assisi's golden boy into God's fool. It took about a dozen, in fact.

To appreciate the hold that social perfectionism had on Francis, it helps to begin with his father, Pietro Bernardone. A shrewd, socially ambitious businessman who used his new money to compensate for his lack of noble blood, Pietro had clear expectations for his son from the start. They began with his name. Pietro wasn't even in the country when Francis was born around 1182—he often traveled for work—but when he returned from France to meet the son his wife had christened John, Pietro renamed him Francis in honor of the country he'd just visited.

It was a telling move. Pietro considered himself the ultimate authority over his wife and children, just as money and social status were the ultimate authorities in his life. He practiced his Catholic faith but not with the fervor of his wife, Pica. Pietro's devotion was to commerce, and he spent long stretches on the road building up the lucrative business he planned to pass on to Francis. That Francis was left behind to be doted on by Pica probably explains how a man as hard and grasping as Pietro could raise a son as genial and happy-go-lucky as Francis.

Francis spent some time in his teens working in his father's cloth shop, but he had no interest in or aptitude for business. It didn't help that he had a habit of giving lavishly to the many beggars who frequented the store when he was working—a habit that infuriated Pietro.

Francis knew he had to do something with his life, something other than sales. So at age twenty, he decided to become a knight. The idea suited his romantic temperament, and when Francis charged off to fight for his hometown in its war against the neighboring city of Perugia, Pietro was pleased. Finally his prodigal son would amount to something.

No sooner had Francis embarked on his first battle than he was captured. He spent a year in a Perugian prison, upbeat as ever as he brokered peace between inmates and bragged about a vision he'd had of his future greatness. He fell ill upon his release in 1203, though, and even after he recovered, something was off. For the first time, Francis sensed a void at the center of his charmed life.

He responded by embarking on another military adventure. Around 1205, Francis dressed himself to the nines, reminded everyone of his dazzling destiny, and galloped out of Assisi to great fanfare with a pack of fellow volunteer soldiers. They were on their way to meet a military commander in Apulia, nearly 400 miles south.

Thirty miles into their journey, the group stopped for the night in Spoleto. Francis came down with a violent fever. As he tossed and turned in bed, he heard an interior voice ask him, "Why are you abandoning the Master for the servant?"

Francis sensed it was the Lord, so he asked what he should do.

"Return to your own city," the voice told him, and await further instructions. That vision of future glory "must be understood differently from the way you have understood it."

A stunned Francis spent the rest of the night in agony, and not only because of the fever. He knew he'd be a laughingstock if he returned to Assisi so soon. It would also spell the end of his military career. But the voice had been unequivocal: The glory God intended for him wasn't on the battlefield. So Francis swallowed hard, and the next morning, he headed home.

After returning to Assisi, as he was riding on the outskirts of town, Francis saw a leper. They weren't hard to spot; medieval lepers had to wear bells warning passersby of their presence, and often you could smell their rotting flesh before you saw them. No one wanted any part of them, least of all vain, fastidious Francis. He always bolted in the opposite direction at the first sign of their contagion.

On this day, though, Francis felt God nudging him not to turn away—to approach the beggar, not from the safety of his horse but from the ground, at eye level.

The idea revolted Francis. Wasn't sharing the same road risky enough? As he had in Spoleto, though, Francis swallowed his squeamishness and resolved to obey. He jumped off his horse, handed the leper some coins, and impulsively kissed the man's gnarled, scabby hand.

The instant he did, Francis felt a bolt of joy surge through his body.

"It was like a somersault," he later told one of his friars, according to biographer Michael de la Bédoyère. "Things that I had thought utterly contrary to my nature suddenly became delightful to me—as delightful to my senses as to my spirit. Soon after that I left the world."

Soon, but not immediately. Kissing the leper freed Francis from his fear of social outcasts. Now he had to face his fear of becoming one himself.

The vague dissatisfaction that Francis had felt from his prison days intensified after his return from Spoleto. His spiritual wake-up calls started coming more frequently, at the least convenient times.

One came in the midst of a blowout street party, where Francis suddenly was struck speechless by longing for God. Friends teased that his bizarre behavior could only be explained by love. He agreed, but dared not tell them Who was wooing his heart.

Another came when Francis took a pilgrimage to Rome. On a whim—or perhaps because he had given all his money to beggars and now had none to get home—he switched clothes with a panhandler and spent the afternoon asking for alms on the steps of St. Peter's Basilica. Francis put on his own clothes again at the end of the day and left the city flooded with joy.

It wasn't long before Francis started sneaking off to a nearby leper colony to taste that supernatural joy on a regular basis. He also began frequenting caves and out-of-the-way chapels, anywhere he could be alone with the Lord. His fear of social shame still dogged him: Once, when praying in the woods, Francis was seized by the certainty that if he didn't drop all this pious nonsense he'd wind up just like that wretched old hunchback woman he'd seen roaming Assisi's streets, the one whose deformities made everyone recoil. Francis shook off the thought and kept on praying.

A year or two after his Spoleto turnaround, Francis was praying in the dilapidated chapel of San Damiano when he heard its Byzantine crucifix speak to him.

"Rebuild My Church," the voice said, "which you can see is falling into ruin."

That this was a summons to found an international religious order and spearhead a revival that would renew the faith of an entire continent had not yet occurred to Francis. He thought God was asking him to renovate a country chapel. So Francis sprung into action, selling his father's horse and a bolt of his best cloth, then hurrying back to give the proceeds to the pastor of San Damiano. The priest took one look at the rich kid's coins and knew what was in store: An angry Pietro soon would be banging on his door, demanding them back.

That's exactly what happened. Although the priest refused the money and Francis began repairing the church by hand, Pietro got wind of his missing goods and flew into a rage. Not only was his son wasting his money, he was making a spectacle of himself—fixing up a chapel no one cared about, begging in the streets for stones for the renovation, hanging out with lepers and bums. Pietro's patience had run out. He rounded up Francis, beat and bound him, and locked him in the family's cellar. Surely a few days spent sitting in the dark and eating only bread and water would be enough to end his coddled son's religious kick.

They weren't. After Pietro left for a business trip and Pica set her son free, Francis went right back to rebuilding his church. He was still scared of his father; he spent a month sleeping in a cave to dodge Pietro, who had begun petitioning civil and religious authorities to recoup the money Francis had taken. But the more Francis prayed and worked on his church and steered clear of his party pals, the freer and bolder he felt. When Assisi's bishop finally summoned him to town to answer his father's charges, Francis once again swallowed hard and obeyed.

The trial took place at the bishop's residence around late 1206, and the whole town gathered to watch. Everyone had been talking about the changes in once-fashionable, fun-loving Francis. Was it true that he had let himself go, that he was gaunt and dirty and living in the streets? Was this another prank or had one of his fevers left him a little loopy? Could Pietro straighten him out?

At the trial, the bishop praised Francis for his generosity but said that even if he intended to use Pietro's money for a good cause, God wouldn't want him to keep it.

Francis agreed, but did the bishop one better.

"I'll gladly give back the money," he said, "and not only my money but my clothes."

At that Francis stripped off his clothes—all of them—and laid them with the coins at his father's feet. Then he turned to face the crowd.

"Listen to me, all of you, and understand. Until now, I have called Pietro Bernardone my father. . . . From now on, I can freely say 'Our Father, who art in heaven,' and not, 'My father, Pietro Bernardone.'"

The audience was stunned. Some wept. Others turned away in disgust. The bishop rushed out of his chair to throw a cloak over nude, shivering Francis.

For his part, Pietro simply scooped up his coins and walked out the door. He never spoke to his son again.

After the trial, Francis spent the next couple of years repairing one countryside chapel after another, begging for his bread, and getting used to life on the margins. It couldn't have been easy for such a jovial extrovert to be cut off from family, mocked and pelted with garbage by street urchins, and assaulted by robbers, as he was shortly after the trial. Nor could it have been easy to renounce worldly success in the same city where he once epitomized it. Begging from strangers is embarrassing enough; begging from former friends who now regard you as the punch line of a bad joke is downright mortifying.

Francis didn't deny the mortification. He accepted it. And slowly, with practice, he learned to embrace it. He reminded himself that Jesus was no stranger to ridicule, that being poor and misunderstood and reviled were experiences the Lord knew well. If Francis truly wanted to live a Christlike life, he couldn't cherry pick the parts of Christ's life he imitated. He had to experience it all: the pain and rejection as well as the freedom and joy. There's no way around the cross, Francis had come to believe. The cross *is* the way.

One February day around 1208, on the feast of Saint Matthias, Francis went to Mass and heard the Gospel reading in which Jesus commissions His disciples, telling them to go from town to town proclaiming the kingdom of God. "Do not take gold or silver or copper for your belts," Jesus says, "no sack for the journey, or a second tunic, or walking stick" (Matt. 10:9–10).

Francis took that passage as his personal marching orders. He ditched his staff on the spot, slipped off his sandals and outer tunic, and traded his belt for a rope. He wasn't called only to repair churches, he realized. He was called to preach the Gospel by living it down to its last detail.

As he did, Francis began to attract a new kind of attention in Assisi. While most people still considered him crazy, a few men noticed his mysterious joy and began wondering if God had a greater purpose for their lives, too. When two of them expressed interest in following him, Francis invited them to join him in searching God's Word for direction.

The three men gathered at the Church of Saint Nicholas and opened the Bible at random three times. The first time, they landed on Matthew 19:21, in which Jesus tells the rich young man, "If you wish to be perfect, go, sell what you have and give to the poor, and you will have treasure in heaven. Then come, follow Me." The second time, they hit Luke 9:3: "Take nothing for the journey, neither walking stick, nor sack, nor food, nor money, and let no one take a second tunic." The third time, they opened to Matthew 16:24: "Whoever wishes to come after Me must deny himself, take up his cross and follow Me."

The message was unmistakable: The Lord was confirming the call He'd given Francis alone a few months earlier, a call that now included others. He was inviting Francis and his followers to literal imitation of the poor man of Nazareth who had "nowhere to rest His head" (Matt. 8:20). As the 1223 Rule of Francis would later explain, they were to "appropriate nothing for themselves, neither a house, nor a place, nor anything else." They were to live, Francis said, "as strangers and pilgrims in the world," just as Peter had advised the early Christians: "Beloved, I urge you as aliens and sojourners to keep away from worldly desires that wage war against the soul" (1 Peter 2:11).

Francis had found his mission, a mission far worthier of his passion and talents than anything he'd envisioned as an aspiring knight. In the ruins of his bondage to social perfectionism, he had discovered the life he was born to lead, a life that would encourage countless conversions, revitalize the Church, and restore the fervor of apostolic times to Christians across Europe.

The Franciscan revolution that began in that little Assisi church eight centuries ago was not confined only to Europe. Its effects also reached the New World—including modern-day California, where eighteenth-century Spanish Franciscan and recently canonized Saint Junípero Serra established a chain of twenty-one missions to spread Christianity to Native Americans. It was in one of those missions where I first felt the pull of Franciscan ideals, albeit indirectly.

I was in my early twenties at the time, on a whirlwind Easter weekend trip to visit my brother and his wife, who were then living in L.A. We had driven up the coast to see the Old Mission Santa Barbara. Built just after Junípero's death and named for a third-century Greek girl who chose to be beheaded rather than renounce her faith, the mission sits on thirteen lush acres overlooking the Pacific and oozing with historical and religious significance.

I had come for the scenery—all the guidebooks said it wasn't to be missed—and maybe also for some direction. My fast-track newspaper career in St. Louis had begun to bore me, and I longed to use my talents to share my newly rekindled faith. Yet I feared taking any drastic steps, knowing that once a writer gets branded as religious, doors close that never reopen.

The internal career debate that had been raging within me all weekend was still going strong as we pulled up to the salmon-colored columns of the mission, but it went mysteriously still within minutes of our arrival. As we began maneuvering through the mission's centuries-old archways and gardens, listening to the birds chirp and breathing the cool air inside its stone chapel, I felt my heart expanding. The sheer beauty of the place—its red-tiled roofs and emerald-green courtyard, its soaring palm trees and fragrant clusters of orange and hot-pink roses, its stark brown cross framed by the Santa Ynez Mountains and a bolt-blue sky—everything seemed to shout to me of God, of His lavish, extravagant, reckless generosity to me. The prospect of giving Jesus control of my career had felt foolish in pallid, still-wintry St. Louis. Here, inside sun-dappled mission walls built by Christians far braver than me, it felt like the logical response to a God so good. It felt natural. And it filled me with joy.

A year after that visit to Santa Barbara, I applied for and won the journalism fellowship that enabled me to leave my newspaper job, write a book about young Christians, and meet my husband. That triple burst of blessings was striking confirmation to me of God's providence. It was also my first grown-up taste of the freedom and joy that come with trading what-will-they-think fears for God's-got-me-covered trust.

Over the course of the next two decades, as I took more steps off the beaten path and visited more Franciscan outposts from Assisi to Mexico City to the Bronx, I gained a deeper appreciation of the saint whose followers built that beautiful mission. I prayed with my mother at the tomb of Francis and his famous, equally fearless follower, Saint Clare, sensing a connection to them that would later result in two of my children—Clara and Joseph Francis—bearing their names. I experienced the healing power of Eucharistic praise-and-worship sessions at the Franciscan University of Steubenville in Ohio, a hub of Catholic revival where the joyful missionary spirit of Francis lives on. I felt a particularly intense draw to Francis while working at the White House, surrounded by powerful people and those desperate to join their ranks. Suddenly inundated with new friends whose interest in me was directly proportional to how much time I'd spent in the West Wing or presidential motorcade that week, I found myself retreating into books about the little poor man of Assisi, longing for a shot of his humility and simplicity in the midst of so much scheming and schmoozing.

When I left the White House and married John, the radical character of Francis and his life became a shared fascination of ours. We knew we weren't called to imitate his literal destitution; we had decent-paying professions, we wanted a family, and purposely choosing to raise our children in a poverty-stricken, high-crime neighborhood for the sake of simplicity, while admirable, felt like more than my nerves could stand. Wimp that I was, though, I knew I didn't want to get sucked into the suburban produce-and-consume cycle that turns family life into a frantic quest to keep up and yields kids who mindlessly parrot pop culture values. John didn't want that either. So we began looking for ways to live our own brand of radical amid an otherwise ordinary life.

Sometimes that quest drove big decisions, like our choice to move to D.C. for my roll-of-the-dice Catholic TV job when prudence would have told us to stay put, or to homeschool our children when it would have been easier and more socially acceptable to send them to school. Sometimes it meant littler or less intuitive choices, like refusing to join the organized sports rat race when it entailed playing games on Sunday, our family day of rest, or tossing our TV shortly after our twins were born (even as I was hosting a TV show) so we'd have more face time with each other and our kids wouldn't waste their childhood staring at screens.

We haven't figured it all out. Nearly every week, something comes up that forces us to decide if we'll do things the conven-

tional way or if God is calling us to break from the pack. The best
choice isn't always clear and it may be decades before we know
whether we're making the right ones. The very act of asking questions is liberating, though. When the pressure is on and everyone
is telling me that I must do *this* thing *this* way at *this* time and if I
don't, my children or I will be irreparably harmed or irredeemably
odd or outright ostracized, it feels good to tune out the hysterics
and ask questions instead. Do I really have to do this? Why? Is
there a better way? And most important: What does God want?

Francis was good at asking those questions. I'm not bad at asking
them myself. But it's in living the answers—boldly and joyfully,
without self-pity or second-guessing or compulsive comparing,
day after day after day—that Francis shone, and I don't.

It's not that I don't act on the answers God gives me. If He
makes His will clear, I do my best to follow. And I usually keep
following in the face of obstacles.

Where I stumble isn't in my execution. It's in my attitude.

I want to follow God cheerfully and confidently as Francis
did, to embrace the countercultural life of a committed Christian
in a secular age without resentment or regret. I know that intentional discipleship, like intentional parenting, will never make
me the world's darling, and that shedding social perfectionism
means accepting that fact with grace and good humor.

Some days, I do that. I'm bright-eyed, undaunted, offering
kind-but-clever rejoinders to those strangers who roll their eyes at
the size of my brood or respond to the news that we homeschool
with one of those "better you than me" quips right in front of my
children. I see old colleagues leapfrogging me in their careers and

thank God for the blessing of spending my days with the children I always wanted and the chance to write about God, even if it never brings me fame or fortune. I feel the flash of awkwardness that comes from not watching the shows others watch or keeping up on social media or the news or fashion trends as they do or having the same automatic sense of community they get from sending their kids to school, and I offer it back to Jesus, knowing that He felt left out long before me.

Then there are the other days, the ones on which everything goes wrong inside my home and out, when the good things I'm trying to do for my family seem to only make life harder for all of us. On those days, it seems that everywhere I turn I face glares from strangers who think I have too many kids or fellow Catholics who wonder why the parochial schools aren't good enough for me or relatives who recoil in horror because my children haven't seen the latest Disney flick. Those are invariably the days that my preschooler doesn't take his nap, my older kids bicker or whine about math, I get a five-alarm work email that I can't respond to because I can't think straight in a house full of hollering kids, and I run into at least three people who tell me what a shame it is that I'm no longer writing newspaper columns or hosting TV shows. If it's a real humdinger of a day, it will end with one of those insufferable cocktail parties where the same people who once crowded around me to find out what I was working on now smile vacantly at the news that I'm writing religious books and home with children. "Most important job in the world," they'll murmur, as they drain the last of their Merlot and scan the room for someone—anyone—more interesting to talk to.

It's on those days that I find myself slipping into bitterness, envy, and sulking. If this is God's will, why doesn't He send me more support? Why does it seem that others who don't give half as much thought to how they spend their time or raise their kids or practice their faith are doing just as well or better than me? Do my efforts to swim against the tide really matter to God or my family? Are they worth the trouble? Or am I a fool who took the narrow road for no reason?

In this death spiral of comparison and negative thinking, I see the true distance between Francis and me—not to mention between Jesus and me. And frankly, it's embarrassing.

Here was Francis, homeless, broke, reviled by nearly everyone who once loved him, and he still managed to sing and dance his way through the byways of Italy, playing a make-believe violin to entertain passing children, waxing poetic to strangers about the goodness of God, and crying grateful tears each time he passed a crucifix. Even as he lay dying, nearly blind and betrayed by friars in his own order who had watered down his founding ideal of absolute poverty, Francis had to be shushed because he was singing so loudly in praise of Jesus. When the friar who tried to quiet him reminded Francis that people expect saints to die somber and silent, not belting out the tunes, Francis smiled. "Oh, let me rejoice in God and praise Him in all my sufferings," he said, then went on singing.

That was Francis. Then there's me, stewing in self-pity because some crank in the hair salon lectured me on population control or because I'm no longer an A-lister at parties I never much cared for anyway. I don't really doubt the decisions I've made; on these matters, at least, God's will for me is clear. I think I'm just irritated that I have to catch flak for my choices, that the world isn't giving me the pat on the back I think I deserve.

Which is, of course, the point. If I pattern my life after the crucified Christ, I should expect the world to give me more kicks in the teeth than pats on the back, at least in this life.

That doesn't mean my life will be one long, insufferable slog up Calvary or that I should adopt a defensive posture. It's tough to be salt and light if you're crouching behind barricades.

What it means, simply, is that I can expect some opposition in the world. If the goal I'm aiming for is different than the one most people are aiming for—if I care more about getting my kids into heaven than into Harvard—then the route I take will be different, too. And I shouldn't be surprised that my refusal to follow the herd attracts a few haters. As Jesus said, "If the world hates you, realize that it hated Me first" (John 15:18). The inverse is also true: If the world loves you and everything you're doing, you can be fairly sure that the god you're serving isn't the One who wound up nailed to a cross.

The temptation, of course, is to waste a lot of time and energy trying to gauge who's serving a false god and who's not, who's embracing the cross like a true believer and who's only in it for the Easter brunches.

Comparisons may be odious, as Teresa of Ávila said, but they're also addictive—particularly for perfectionists. We like to succeed, and sometimes it seems the only way to know if we're succeeding at something as nebulous as living our faith or raising our children is to find someone else attempting the same and falling short. It's as if we think God is grading on a curve and if enough other souls rank behind us, we'll pass the test.

If only it were that easy. The reality is that God judges me on fidelity to my calling, not to anyone else's, and I can never fully know what's happening inside another life or heart. Which probably explains why comparing myself to others leaves me more miserable than inspired. Either I enjoy a brief flash of superiority before realizing that I've fallen into the sin of presumption, or I feel jealous and defeated at the discovery that I'm lagging behind. Neither experience leads me closer to Jesus or to joy.

Maybe that's why Francis had no use for comparisons. He told his friars never to judge the rich "but rather let everyone judge and despise himself." As for envy, he considered it a flirtation with blasphemy, since God is the Author of all good and envying another person the good in his life is tantamount to envying God Himself. Francis didn't even want his followers to compare themselves to him. "I have done what was mine to do," he said near the end of his life. "May Christ teach you what is yours."

Francis practiced what he preached. His post-conversion life was a study in tuning out the distractions of comparison, concern for reputation, regrets, and all the rest. It wasn't that he didn't notice other people or their opinions; he simply cared more about the opinion of God. His was, as author Patti Normile puts it, "a way of spiritual subtraction": a spirituality that was less about rejecting the world than about focusing so intently on God's will that he didn't have any attention left over for lesser concerns.

Many of us have had moments when we felt seized by single-minded passion for Christ, usually on the heels of a conversion. The remarkable thing about Francis is that his passion never let go; he retained it to the day he died. That initial fire of conversion grew only hotter as the years passed, until it finally burned away nearly everything in his life and soul that wasn't of God.

In the midst of that holy fire, there was no room to look

around at other people or behind at other roads he might have taken. There wasn't even room to look at his own good works. "Nothing but our vices and sins belong to us," Francis liked to say. Or as he put it to his friars shortly before his death, "Let us begin again, for up to now, we have done nothing."

For Francis, the only direction to look was forward, at Jesus. He saw each day as a new opportunity to follow Christ more closely, to live more fully the Beatitudes that are the clearest standard of perfection that Jesus gives in the Gospels.

The poverty of spirit for which Francis was famous wasn't the poverty of a world-hating stoic or a spacy ascetic lost in a trance. It was the poverty of a pilgrim, a man who knew he couldn't get where he wanted to go unless he traveled light.

Last spring, eighteen years after my first visit to the Old Mission Santa Barbara, I returned with my husband and children.

It was as gorgeous as I remembered. The birds were singing, the roses were blooming, and stunning mountain and ocean vistas competed for our admiration with newly restored stonework on the mission's façade. Unlike most other nostalgia trips I've led my family on, this one lived up to its billing.

It was one of seven missions we visited that vacation. I'd always wanted to take a trip to see all twenty-one, but with four kids in tow—including one still taking naps—I was happy to settle for a third of them. I was even happier to have found time before the trip to read up on Junípero Serra. I wanted to learn more about this intrepid little Franciscan priest who traded a prestigious post as chair of a university theology department in Spain for a harrowing overseas adventure in the American wilderness. I sensed he had something of the spark of Francis in him, that same thirst to pursue Gospel perfection at any price.

What I read confirmed my hunch. Junípero was an unlikely missionary: Five-foot-two, skinny, and prone to asthma, he was over the hill by the standards of his day (he sailed from Spain at age thirty-five and didn't found his first mission until age fifty-six). Yet Junípero volunteered himself anyway. He felt his faith atrophying in academia and wanted "to revive in my soul those intense longings which I have had since my novitiate when I read the lives of the saints." Junípero knew his loved ones would not understand, especially his aging parents, whom he'd never see again. "Tell them how badly I feel at not being able to stay longer and make them happy as I used to do," Junípero wrote in a farewell letter to a friend, before adding: "first things must come first; and our first duty, undoubtedly, is to do the will of God."

Over the next few decades, that single-minded fidelity to God's will fortified Junípero through hunger, scurvy, bad weather, dangerous terrain, violent attacks from some of the native Californians, political battles with Spanish government and military officials, and his own failing health—including a crippled left leg that he wounded shortly after arriving in the New World. It's estimated that he walked some ten thousand miles up and down the coast preaching the Gospel, establishing missions, and administering the sacraments. A true son of Francis, Junípero packed only the essentials, sleeping on the ground during his trips with a foot-long crucifix spread across his chest. He finally died of likely heart failure at age seventy, after an exhausting three-year, six hundred-mile trek to administer the sacrament of Confirmation to thousands of new Christians at every mission from San Diego to San Francisco.

Junípero's canonization by Pope Francis in 2015 was controversial. Critics say his mission system was paternalistic and oppressive. Supporters say his love and sacrifices for the Native Americans whom he called "the reasonable people" made him one of their few advocates in a Spanish colonial system that too often treated them as subhuman.

For me, the most pressing question about Junípero is why he went to California at all, and why he stayed despite such opposition. I can understand leaving comfort, prestige, and popularity when missionary fervor first strikes. But sticking with it for the rest of your life when every day is harder than the next and almost no one has your back? How did he do that? How does anyone?

I think the answer has something to do with Junípero's famous motto, the one we saw displayed at every mission we visited. It's an echo of that line from Francis instructing his friars to "pass through the world like pilgrims and strangers." Junípero's version is simpler still: "Always forward, never back."

The first time I heard that motto, I thought it was about pluck and tenacity: No matter what befalls you, keep forging ahead. But the more I've read about Junípero's life and reflected on the legacy of his spiritual father, Francis, the more I've come to believe that it's about something deeper and more demanding. I think it's about packing light as we move through life, leaving behind the baggage of "what if," "why me," and "what will they say" so we can freely seek the answer to the only question that really counts: "What is God asking of me right now?"

So much of perfectionism is about looking in the wrong direction: at the world and its expectations, at others and their choices, at myself and my fears and flaws. It's about looking backward at mistakes and regrets, or sideways at other paths I might have taken. It's about looking everywhere except where my eyes actually belong: fixed on Jesus, the true perfecter of my faith.

Not looking in the wrong direction in this life is hard; it's like not thinking of a hot-fudge sundae while standing in line at Baskin-Robbins on last day of Lent. The only way to avoid the temptation is to look at something better, to stay in forward spiritual motion so I don't get stuck on something less. It's what Jesus told Peter to do when Peter was peppering Him with nosy questions about what He had in store for the other apostles. "What concern is it of yours?" Jesus answered. "You follow Me" (John 21: 22).

Follow Me.

Seek the city that is to come.

Always forward, never back.

Francis knew all this. It's the reason his breaks with the world were so dramatic and decisive, the reason he ditched his clothes as well as his coins, the reason he embraced the literal poverty that freed him to achieve the even more elusive poverty of spirit Jesus calls for in the Beatitudes. Francis knew he couldn't trade his prosthetic life for a prophetic one without making big changes, the kind the world could see and, yes, ridicule. Francis knew the Christian life isn't a Sunday stroll; it's a race. And like Paul, Francis wasn't content to go with the flow or settle for good enough. He wanted to "run so as to win" (1 Cor. 9:24).

The other day, as I was cleaning out our minivan after a long car ride, I found a scrap of paper under my seat. It was a drawing of an arresting, angular figure, a man wearing all brown, with lips pursed in concentration and huge saucer eyes staring off at a point in the distance. Above his head, in blue pen, were scrawled the words "Junípero Serra."

The name was spelled perfectly; even the accent was in the right spot. And on the back of the picture was this message, in the handwriting of my eight-year-old John Patrick: "Always forward, never back."

It's funny, because as much as I've been thinking about Junípero and his motto lately, I don't think I've mentioned him to John Patrick since our trip to the missions a year ago. Maybe the saint was on his mind because of the children's book about him on our shelf, or because the kids have taken to occasionally chanting "always forward, never back" during our hikes, or because seeing seven missions in ten days is enough to burn anything into a child's memory. We did our best to intersperse those visits with playtime and beach jaunts, but there were a few groans of *"another one?"* near the end. John Patrick's were among the loudest.

And yet here he is, internalizing a motto I wish I'd learned decades ago, a motto I'm only beginning to understand in my forties. It makes me glad that we saw more than seals and redwoods on that trip, glad that I have photos not only of amazing sunsets and smiling kids but of those kids standing before crosses and chapels and mission walls.

My favorite photo from that trip is one we took after Mass at the San Buenaventura Mission. Our children are wearing their Sunday best, their clothes slightly rumpled from the heat but not yet as sullied as they will be once they discover the lizards they can chase through the mission's garden or the irresistible lure of its fountain. They're clustered together in front of an old olive press—three-year-old Joseph Francis is actually perched on top of the press, looking slightly defiant because he knows I'm about to tell him to get down. Clara and Maryrose are standing beneath him, smiling sweetly for the camera.

John Patrick, meanwhile, is standing off to the side and squinting in curiosity at a hand-painted wooden sign over his right shoulder. In neatly printed yellow capitals, it reads:

ONLY ONE LIFE

TWILL SOON BE PAST

ONLY WHAT'S DONE FOR CHRIST WILL LAST

I smile to think of my son mulling over those words, of this little boy who shares my late father's middle name turning them over in his mind and tucking them away among those childhood memories that resurface at the most surprising times. And I like to think that somewhere, Francis and Junípero and my dad are smiling, too.

8

FROM HEAD TO HEART

I slept, but my heart was awake.
A sound! My beloved is knocking.
"Open to me, my sister, my love,
   my dove, my perfect one . . ."
My beloved put his hand to the latch,
and my heart was thrilled within me.
I arose to open to my beloved . . .

(Song of Songs 5:2a, 4–5a)

On the night of my wedding, an old friend of my husband stood up to toast us. I can't recall most of what he said. I think he cracked a few jokes about their hijinks together in youth group at Peoria's First United Methodist Church. Maybe he complimented us as a couple. Then, just as I was preparing to swig my bubbly on cue at the toast's predictable "May you live happily ever after" finale, the boyish-faced father of five raised his glass and said this:

"May the Lord break both your hearts."

I think I choked on my champagne.

I recovered quickly enough, smiling and waving thanks for what I knew was a well-intentioned, if buzz-killing, sentiment. I figured it was one of those phrases that our evangelical friends and relatives understood better than a cradle Catholic like me. I made a mental note to ask John about it later. In the excitement of the evening, I soon forgot.

Yet as the years passed and my wedding memories faded, those words never did. I'd be drying dishes or driving down the highway and suddenly I'd hear them rattling around in my brain, reverberating almost like a curse: *May the Lord break both your hearts.* I'd picture him saying them to us, his eyes filled with light and some wisdom I hadn't yet gleaned, and I'd wonder: What did he mean by that? What value is there in a broken heart—for us or anyone?

I knew suffering was inevitable in marriage, as in all of life. I also knew it could be redemptive. My father had taught me that, through the Alzheimer's battle that ended five years after we swayed together on that parquet dance floor, my wedding gown rustling as Dad crooned "Sunrise, Sunset" in my ear. In those last years of Dad's life, I saw his faith and love grow only brighter as his strength and independence ebbed.

Still, I didn't envision Dad suffering from a broken heart so much as a humbled intellect and a stretched soul. And even as I began moving through my own grown-up trials—including a four-year battle with infertility that would become the defining experience of our young marriage—I didn't warm to the image of a broken heart. Enduring suffering, offering it up to Jesus, finding God's joy in the midst of it: Those I could understand. But welcoming, even praying for a wounded and broken heart? Why would I ever want to do that?

Over the last few years, as I've immersed myself in the stories and struggles of recovering perfectionist saints, I've been struck by how many different types of people walked this path before me. They were soldiers and scholars, bishops and beggars, mothers and monks. Some perfectionist saints were studious and scrupulous; others were congenital romantics or compulsive worker bees.

There's one thing nearly all of them had in common, though. Almost to a person, they were intensely devoted to the heart of Jesus.

I know that can sound strange if you're not Catholic—or if you are, but you're as clueless about such things as I once was. How can someone be devoted to a particular body part of Jesus? And why His heart? Why not His face or His foot or His left elbow?

Unpacking the mystery and apparent oddness of what's known as the Sacred Heart devotion was never a project that particularly interested me before I started studying perfectionist saints. I'd seen Sacred Heart images since I was a child: those soft-focus portraits of a sad-eyed, slightly androgynous figure pointing to an exposed, blood-red heart. That heart was usually encircled by thorns, pierced by a lance or dripping with blood, and almost always crowned with tongues of fire and a cross.

The pictures were maudlin. And they did nothing for me.

It's not that I didn't feel a twinge of sorrow when I'd see them, particularly when I was a little girl and I'd spot them on a holy card or hanging in the church vestibule just after I'd nursed an ugly thought about my older brother or repeated some schoolyard gossip. I'd see those big sad eyes of my Savior and think, for a minute, how much Jesus suffered for me and how ungrateful I was in return.

As I grew older, Sacred Heart images became like so much wallpaper in the background of my spiritual life. No one ever explained their meaning to me, and it was hard not to feel manipulated by their mawkishness. Who wants to look at a picture calculated to make you feel guilty and sad? Aren't we all a little beyond that pre-Vatican II Catholic kitsch?

Then one night, when I was twenty-four and still fresh from that altar-call experience at the charismatic Mass in St. Louis, I stepped into the field house of Franciscan University of Steubenville and saw the Sacred Heart of Jesus as if for the first time.

The portrait, by an unknown eighteenth-century artist, was elevated on a stand near the front of the auditorium, in a place where I could see it even from behind a massive crowd of swaying, praying young adults. It had no pastels or gauzy halos. Its background was black and the bust of its realistic, gaunt-yet-masculine Christ emerged as from a shadow.

This Jesus faced me head-on, with tears streaking His scratched-up cheeks and a clear, determined look in His eyes. His exposed heart was there but He wasn't holding it. He wasn't doing anything, really. He was just looking at me and letting me look at Him. Beneath His heart, in Latin, were the first few words of John 3:16: *For God so loved the world.*

I'd seen this picture before, when I had visited Steubenville a couple years earlier for a weekend conference. Back then I had barely noticed it.

But on this night, at the end of a two-week private retreat I'd taken to reconnect with God, in the midst of hundreds of young men and women singing praise songs as they adored Jesus in the Eucharist, it overpowered me. I dropped to my knees, tears escaping my eyes as I looked, simply looked, at this God who loved me enough to give me His own body and blood, who loved me enough to die for me.

When I left Steubenville the next day, I bought a framed copy of that portrait to hang in the center of my apartment. It has hung in the center of every home I've lived in since. Even today, if you walk in the front door of my house, those piercing eyes of Jesus, and His crimson, fire-tinged heart, are the first things you'll see.

Ask me to explain that picture to you, though, and I'll have some trouble. Or at least I would have had trouble until very recently.

My study of recovering perfectionist saints convinced me that I needed to understand what it was, exactly, that spoke to them about the Sacred Heart—what had spoken to me that night in Steubenville. Why did so many saints see meditating on and imitating the heart of Jesus as the key to their victory over perfectionism? Why did so many perfectionist heretics, like the Jansenists, harbor special hatred for this devotion? What do Scripture and the Church Fathers have to say about the relationship between God's heart and ours?

And what does any of this have to do with overcoming perfectionism?

Even before I dug into God's Word and church history with those questions, I sensed their answers had something to do with that part of the Sermon on the Mount that has always haunted me as a spiritual perfectionist. It's the passage where Jesus spells out exactly what it takes to achieve Christian perfection, in terms clearer than any others He uses in Scripture aside from His sell-it-all advice to the rich young man:

> "You have heard that it was said, 'You shall love your neighbor and hate your enemy.' But I say to you, love your enemies, and pray for those who persecute you, that you may be children of your heavenly Father, for He makes His sun rise on the bad and the good, and causes rain to fall on the just and the unjust. For if you love those who love you, what recompense will you have? Do not the tax collectors do the same? And if you greet your brothers only, what is unusual about that? Do not the pagans do the same? So be perfect, just as your heavenly Father is perfect" (Matt. 5:43–48).

To be perfect, Jesus seems to say, is to love others even when they hurt us, and to keep loving them even when they keep hurting us. To be perfect is to love as God loves.

It's a daunting standard. And the more I learn about how perfectionism has shaped my life and personality, the more daunting it seems.

When you're buried in the pit of perfectionism, you think you have a fighting chance of clawing your way toward this sort of limitless, all-merciful love. When you're halfway out, though, the view changes. You begin to look around and realize how disoriented you were and how far you still have to go to reach freedom. You start to see your life in a new and less flattering light: the people and events that taught you as a child that you had to be perfect to be loved; the opportunists who later spotted your perfectionism and exploited it for their own purposes; the mistakes you made with your own children before you realized you were making them—and those you keep on making even after you know better.

All this reconsidering and reassessing can lead to resentment, even rage, and grief. You feel overwhelmed by the damage done to you and the damage you've done to others, by the realization that you might be fighting this battle for the rest of your life. Maybe you even feel angry at God, as you ask questions that seem to have no answers: *Why did You let me fall into this pit when I was too young to know better? Why aren't You parachuting me out now?*

At this stage of the journey, when you see clearly how much needs pardoning in yourself and in others, forgiveness no longer seems hard; it seems impossible. Loving as heedlessly as God loves feels like a fool's move, a ticket only to more pain. And all those baby steps you've taken—toward embracing gentleness and patience, stalking joy and rejecting fear, growing in discernment and balance and freedom from the world's expectations—seem to pale in comparison with the monumental task that looms ahead: the task of learning to love and forgive perfectly, as God does.

All of which brings us back to the Sacred Heart. The saints faced the same temptations to cynicism, despondency, and despair that we face. They saw their limits as clearly as we see ours—more clearly, in fact. And they had plenty of reasons to play the victim or play it safe.

Yet the saints chose vulnerability over vindictiveness. They chose to keep their wounded hearts wide open, like Christ's, to keep loving no matter how many times the world or even their own family and friends hurt them. They chose to draw near to God in their suffering rather than to blame Him for it—not once, but again and again and again.

Their devotion to the Sacred Heart of Jesus helped them make those choices. Reflecting on and drawing near to the heart of Jesus can help us, too, as we seek to escape the final and most pernicious trap of perfectionism: the temptations of stuckness and self-protection, of refusing to forgive others and ourselves for the wounds unearthed on this journey.

Those wounds tempt us to believe that the cool, guarded heart of a perfectionist is our only sure fortress in this fallen world. The surprising truth that the saints discovered—that real strength and resilience are found only in hearts broken open by love—can set us free. First, though, we must enter into the mystery of the most loving heart ever to beat inside a human body: the pierced and broken heart of Jesus Christ.

Like those schmaltzy Sacred Heart images I never much liked as a child, the word "heart" has a tendency to seem trite. That's partly because its literal meaning—a crucial organ that pumps blood to our bodies and sustains our lives—bears so little resemblance to its figurative meaning in today's pop culture, which treats "heart" as synonymous with "feelings."

Heart has a different, far deeper meaning in Scripture. The word appears some eight hundred times in the Old and New Testaments, and while its biblical meaning touches on both modern definitions—the heart as wellspring of life and the heart as seat of emotions—it also goes beyond them. In the Word of God, your heart is not merely a part of you, another physical appendage or aspect of your personality. The heart is you: your deepest identity, the center of your spiritual, emotional, and moral life, the place where you make decisions and judgments. The heart is your core.

It's no wonder, then, that God spends so much of Scripture calling us to a change of heart. Beginning as early as Genesis, where we read that the evil desires of the human heart grieved the heart of God (Gen. 6:5–6), we find continual reminders that God has a heart and He wants us to imitate it.

We see this in the First Book of Samuel, where the Lord seeks "a man after His own heart to appoint as ruler" (1 Sam. 13:14), and finds him not in the older, more strapping sons of Jesse but in the younger, forgotten David. "People look at the outward appearance," God tells Samuel, "but the Lord looks at the heart" (1 Sam. 16:7).

When God lays out His Commandments, the first—and greatest, as Jesus reminds us—concerns the heart: "You shall love the Lord, your God, with your whole heart, and with your whole being, and with your whole strength" (Deut. 6:5, Mark 12:30). God doesn't just communicate His law to the minds of His people; He writes it "on their hearts" (Jer. 31:33, Rom. 2:15). He does that because the heart, as Jesus explains, is the locus of good and evil in a person: "From within people, from their hearts, come evil thoughts, unchastity, theft, murder, adultery, greed, malice, deceit, licentiousness, envy, blasphemy, arrogance, folly" (Mark 7:21–22).

So what does it mean to have hearts that look like God's, "hearts that do not condemn us" (1 John 3:21) but that please the Lord who promises to "test the heart" (Jer. 17:10)? We know we must be "pure of heart" to see God (Matt. 5:8), but what else does God want to see in our hearts besides laser-focused love for Him and obedience to His law?

The answer, I'd argue, is vulnerability.

Over and over in Scripture, when hearts are praised, they are praised for openness, warmth, even a willingness to be wounded. The hearts that God celebrates are those humble enough to recognize their need for His mercy and generous enough to extend that mercy to others. "You do not desire sacrifice," the psalmist writes, but "a contrite, humbled heart, O God, you will not scorn" (Ps. 51:18–19). Wide-open, wounded hearts draw God like a magnet: "The Lord is close to the brokenhearted, those who are crushed in spirit He saves" (Ps. 34:19).

In his letters, Paul urges us to be "tenderhearted, forgiving one another, as God in Christ forgave you" (Eph. 4:32). He describes his own heart as filled with "great sorrow and constant anguish" over the plight of those who have persecuted him, even going so far as to wish that he could be separated from God if that would save their souls (Rom. 9:2–3).

That mix of anguish and tenderness is one Jesus knew well. He weeps over the fate of the city where He will be crucified (Luke 19:41) and His heart is "moved with pity" for the very crowds that He knows will turn against Him (Mark 6:34, Matt. 9:36). In the Gospel passage where Jesus describes His own heart most explicitly, He highlights His vulnerability, not His strength: "Take My yoke upon you, and learn from Me, for I am gentle and lowly in heart" (Matt. 11:29). When it's time to convince the apostles of His identity, Jesus doesn't flex His muscles; He bears His wounds: "Then He said to Thomas, 'Put your finger here and see My hands, and bring your hand and put it into My side, and do not be unbelieving, but believe'" (John 20:27).

Divinity didn't protect Jesus from heartbreak. Even as one of His apostles was resting on His heart at the Last Supper, Jesus was "deeply troubled" because another was plotting His betrayal

(John 13:21–26). The lance that pierced Christ's heart on the cross, allowing blood and water to pour out on those He had already forgiven (John 19:34, Luke 23:34), reminds us of the heartache Christ experienced at our rejection, and even more, at our indifference.

Indifference, coldness, a guarded or grudging heart—few qualities come in for more fervent or frequent rebukes in Scripture than these. The Lord repeatedly warns His people about the danger of a heart hardened by stubbornness (1 Sam. 6:6), unforgiveness (Matt. 18:35), or sin and worry (Luke 21:34). An insensitive heart may be wounded less, but as Jesus reminds us, it's also less likely to be healed:

> *"For this people's heart has grown dull, and their ears are hard of hearing, and they have shut their eyes; so that they might not look with their eyes, and listen with their ears, and understand with their heart and turn—and I would heal them" (Matt. 13:15, cf. Isa. 6:9–10).*

The healing Jesus offers for our hearts is less repair surgery than full-on transplant. Since God is love (1 John 4:8), the only way we can truly love like God—fully, freely, fearlessly—is to love with a new heart, His heart. It's a gift the Lord longs to give us: "I will give you a new heart, and a new spirit I will put within you. I will remove the heart of stone from your flesh and give you a heart of flesh" (Ezek. 36:26).

This gift comes with risks, the greatest being a share in the same pain, betrayal, and ingratitude that Jesus faced. When Paul declares that "it is no longer I who live, but it is Christ who lives in me," he prefaces that statement with a reminder of what it cost to let the Lord live and love in him: "I have been crucified with Christ" (Gal.

2:19–20). To have the heart of Christ is to have a broken heart, the heart of a man who "was spurned and avoided by men . . . pierced for our sins and crushed for our iniquity" (Isa. 53:3, 5).

Most perfectionists, and most anyone, would prefer to share in the power and glory of the risen Christ. Those, too, are attributes of God. But God chooses to reveal His power in human weakness (2 Cor. 12:9). Accepting the gift of God's heart means allowing His chosen way to be our way, too.

If we do that, we not only inch closer to the ideal of loving others more perfectly. Paul says we also discover how perfectly we ourselves are loved. As he reminds the Ephesians, it's only when Christ "dwell(s) in your hearts through faith; that you, rooted and grounded in love, may have strength to comprehend with all the holy ones what is the breadth and length and height and depth, and to know the love of Christ that surpasses knowledge . . ." (Eph. 3:17–19).

In other words, a heart united to God's knows its true worth. It's a heart full enough and brave enough to open wide to a hurting world—and to stay open, for good.

The list of holy ones who recognized and wrote about the power hidden in the heart of Christ stretches back to the earliest days of the Church. It includes more than a dozen Church Fathers and nearly every recovering perfectionist saint we've met in this book.

That list begins with such second- and third-century Christians as Saint Justin the Martyr, Saint Irenaeus, Tertullian, and Hippolytus of Rome, as well as later Church Fathers such as Saint

Ambrose, Saint Augustine, and Saint John Chrysostom. As theologian Timothy T. O'Donnell documents in his sweeping study, *Heart of the Redeemer*, these early Christians saw great meaning in the blood and water that flowed from Christ's side on the cross (John 19:34), often identifying that blood and water with the "living water" of grace that Jesus promised would flow from His heart (John 7:38).

That living water gives life to our souls, particularly through the sacraments of baptism (water) and the Eucharist (blood). It also gives life to the Church, which Augustine describes as born from the pierced side of Christ: "while the Lord slept on the cross, His side was transfixed with a spear, and the sacraments flowed forth, whence the Church was born." Justin, writing three centuries earlier, concludes the same: "We Christians are the true Israel which springs from Christ, for we are drawn out of His heart as out of a rock."

The Church Fathers also saw significance in John 13:23, where Saint John—"the Apostle of Love"—rests on Christ's breast, or heart. Saint Paulinus describes John as drinking "Wisdom from the Heart of all-creating Wisdom," while Augustine says John "drew loftier mysteries from [Christ's] inmost heart," a gift that enabled him to write his mystical "Gospel of Love." Noting these and other patristic references in his book, *A Heart on Fire*, Jesuit James Kubicki says early Christians saw John as a symbol of the Church, which is called to draw near to the heart of the Lord and receive from it the same supernatural strength that enabled John to stay by Christ's side after all the other apostles fled.

The focus on Christ's wounded heart that we see among the Church Fathers was a powerful antidote to early heresies that denied Christ's full humanity. O'Donnell notes that already by the third century, Christians in Rome were being urged to meditate on the pierced side of Christ at 3 p.m., the hour when Jesus died on the cross. That practice probably rankled such perfectionist heretics as the body-hating Gnostics (or "the perfect," as they sometimes called themselves), the Docetists, and the Monophysitists, all of whom found the idea of salvation through a suffering God-made-man too scandalous to bear.

Devotion to the pierced heart of Jesus probably also repelled the perfectionist Pelagians whom Augustine battled in the fifth century. While the Pelagians were denying original sin and our need for redemption in Christ, treating His suffering on the cross as merely a good example for us to follow while we work our way to heaven, Augustine was championing the necessity of Christ's sacrificial death for our salvation. And along with Paulinus, John Chrysostom, and others, Augustine was pointing to the pierced heart of Jesus as an object lesson in the humble, saving love of God: "Are not all the treasures of wisdom and knowledge hidden in You reduced to this, that we learn from You as something great that You are meek and humble of heart?"

These early seeds grew into a robust and widespread devotion to the heart of Jesus in the Middle Ages, mostly through Benedictine saints and theologians. While Benedict himself makes no explicit mention of the Sacred Heart, his Rule focuses heavily on heart change and includes nearly three dozen references to our hearts, starting with an opening line that paraphrases Proverbs 4:20 ("incline your ear to my sayings") but with a typical Benedictine spin: "incline the ear of your heart."

That attention to the biblical concept of metanoia—or change of heart—probably primed Benedictines such as Saint

Bernard of Clairvaux and Saint Gertrude the Great for their well-known devotion to the Sacred Heart. Gertrude was one of several thirteenth-century Benedictine women mystics who spoke of offering their hearts to Jesus or exchanging their hearts for His, praying, as Gertrude does in her *Spiritual Exercises*, that Jesus would "absorb my heart totally in You." Bernard, a twelfth-century abbot, prayed that the heart of Christ would cleanse his own, make it warmer and more tender, and "pierce" him with God's love. "Unite my heart with Yours," he begs, "and let Your wounded love be found in my heart."

Love for Christ's wounds was a major focus of Francis of Assisi, whose devotion to the suffering Christ began at the base of the San Damiano crucifix around 1206 and went on to mark his entire life and spirituality, not to mention his body. In describing Francis' experience of the stigmata, thirteenth-century Franciscan theologian Saint Bonaventure—himself an ardent proponent of the Sacred Heart devotion—says God helped Francis understand that "he was to be totally transformed into the likeness of Christ crucified, not by the martyrdom of his flesh, but by the fire of [Christ's] love consuming his soul." The heart of Francis was wounded as Christ's was, Bonaventure says, and that wounding filled Francis with love.

The links between early perfectionist saints and the heart of Christ are discernable, if indirect. Once we reach the seventeenth century, though, evidence of devotion to the Sacred Heart among ex-perfectionist saints is obvious and overwhelming.

Two of the clearest examples are Francis de Sales and Jane de Chantal, who took as the emblem of their Visitation Order an image of the pierced heart of Jesus. As Francis writes in a letter to Jane, "Our little congregation is the work of the Hearts of Jesus and Mary. Our dying Savior gave birth to us by the wound in His Sacred Heart."

In an era of cold moralism, Francis and Jane wanted their Visitation sisters to be women whose hearts burned with divine love—women like Mary, who continually "pondered . . . in her heart" the mystery of Her Son and allowed her own heart to be "pierced by the sword" of His suffering (Luke 2:19, 35). "Put your whole heart entirely into the hands of God," Jane tells her daughter, repeating advice she frequently gave her nuns. Francis tells his spiritual directees that if they cultivate a Christlike heart, virtue will follow: "As our beloved Jesus lives in your heart, so, too, He will live in your conduct and He will be revealed by your eyes, mouth, hands, yes even the hair on your head."

So how do we welcome Jesus into our hearts? By bearing patiently and lovingly with suffering, Francis says, including life's little annoyances: "the headache, or toothache, or heavy cold; the tiresome peculiarities of husband or wife, the broken glass, the loss of a ring . . . the sneer of a neighbor," all of which can yield "spiritual riches" and a heart more conformed to Christ's. When we don't manage such forbearance, Francis says, "Hide your heart gently in our Lord's wounds, without making any vehement effort; have great confidence that in His mercy and goodness He will not forsake you . . ."

This process of uniting our hearts to Christ's, and opening our wounds to Him for healing, begins anew each day. Stumbles and setbacks are inevitable; what counts is how often we get back up. As Francis tells a mother frustrated by her stubborn faults,

Starting in the morning, prepare your heart for peace; take great care throughout the day to call it back often to that peace and to take your heart again in your hand. If you do something that causes you distress, do not let it scare you, by no means trouble yourself; but, having recognized [your fault], humble yourself gently before God and try to restore your spirit to an attitude of calm.

Jane knew the wisdom of that advice firsthand, having used it to overcome her own frustration and fiery temper. The most memorable phrases of her letters reveal a similar moment-by-moment, heart-centered spirituality: "God only wants our heart"; "Keep your heart firmly set on God, and casting out all that is not He"; "Put yourself before God very simply . . . [and] gently pour into His Sacred Heart whatever your own heart bids you to say."

Jane was living proof that grace can transform deep wounds into deep joy. The combination of her husband's death and her in-laws' abuse could have trapped her forever in victimhood and vindictiveness had she not opened her wounds to Christ's healing touch. As Jane reminds her fellow perfectionists, Jesus heals even our self-inflicted wounds of sin:

When you have fallen into some fault, go to God with a humble spirit, saying to Him: "I have sinned, my God, I am sorry"; then, with loving trust, add: "Father, pour the oil of Your abundant mercy on my wounds, for You are my only hope, heal me."

Given the emphasis on wounded hearts in the spirituality of Francis and Jane, it's no wonder that the saint most famously associated with the Sacred Heart devotion hailed from the order they founded. Saint Margaret Mary Alacoque, a French Visitation nun born twenty-five years after Francis died and five years after the death of Jane, experienced a series of visions centered on the heart of Jesus. Those visions began on the feast of John the Apostle in 1673 and included a mystical experience of exchanging her heart for the heart of Christ.

Despite great resistance from skeptics both inside and outside her convent, and thanks largely to the support of her Jesuit confessor, Saint Claude de la Colombière, this private gift to Margaret Mary became a blessing for the whole Church. The Sacred Heart devotion nurtured in her soul spread first through her convent, then to other Visitation convents, and finally—with the help of popular books written by her Jesuit spiritual director John Croiset and another Jesuit priest, Joseph de Galliffet—to Christians throughout the world.

It's fitting that the spiritual sons of Ignatius of Loyola played a key role in Margaret Mary's mission, given the importance of the heart in Ignatian spirituality. The discernment method that had helped the founder of the Jesuits overcome his perfectionism more than a century earlier sprang from the realization that God speaks to us through the movements of our hearts. Ignatius arrived at that epiphany in the midst of his sickbed conversion as a young soldier. It wasn't analyzing a theological treatise that changed Ignatius; it was entering imaginatively into stories of Christ and the saints. His was a heart change.

In his *Spiritual Exercises*, Ignatius encourages use of the imagination in prayer and Scripture study, so that the Word of God can speak to our hearts as well as our minds. He explains, "For it is not knowing much, but realizing and relishing things interiorly, that contents and satisfies the soul." One sure way to "relish . . . interiorly" the truths of our faith is to meditate on the vulnerable, pierced body of our Lord. In his most famous prayer, the Anima Christi (Soul of Christ), Ignatius explicitly asks to enter into the woundedness of Jesus:

> Soul of Christ, sanctify me
> Body of Christ, save me
> Blood of Christ, inebriate me
> Water from the side of Christ, wash me
> Passion of Christ, strengthen me
> O Good Jesus, hear me
> Within Your wounds hide me . . .

The earthy, incarnational bent of Ignatian spirituality, and its strong emphasis on the heart, made the Jesuits natural allies of the Sacred Heart devotion. And that made them natural enemies of the perfectionist Jansenists, who were determined to snuff it out.

Everything that made the heart of Jesus a refuge for recovering perfectionists made it a threat to the Jansenist worldview. The Sacred Heart symbolized God's nearness and mercy; Jansenists stressed His distance and severity. The Sacred Heart showed a God burning with love for us and longing for our love in return; the Jansenists saw God as stingy with His saving grace and unimpressed by anything we do. The Sacred Heart reminded us of God's self-emptying, universal love; the Jansenists worshipped a savior whose concern was limited to a narrow elect, the ranks of whom most Christians couldn't even hope to join.

There was something else, too: Although Jansenists professed belief in the Incarnation, the sheer physicality of Sacred Heart images—and the revulsion Jansenists expressed at them—exposed the shallowness of that belief. Pictures of the Sacred Heart of Jesus force us to reckon with the full implications of a God who became one of us, and for Jansenists, those implications were troubling. If the King of the universe took the form of a slave (Phil. 2:7) and allowed His heart to be wounded so we could be healed (1 Pet. 2:24), if even Christ's risen body still bears the marks of His wounds (John 20:20), then denying or hiding our wounds, or lamenting that we have them in the first place, makes little sense. And a perfectionist theology that prods us to hate weakness in ourselves and others, or white-knuckle our way to salvation, starts to seem a little ludicrous.

The Jansenists recognized the threat that the Sacred Heart devotion posed and they took to deriding its proponents as "heart worshippers." They argued that focusing on Christ's heart exalted His humanity at the expense of His divinity—a claim that conveniently ignored the millennia-old biblical tradition of treating the heart as a symbol of the whole person.

As the eighteenth century wore on and the battle between Jansenists and Jesuits heated up, another recovering perfectionist entered the fray. It was Alphonsus Liguori, the bishop, moral theologian, and hard-core scruples sufferer whose freedom from perfectionist fear had come through intense focus on God's merciful love. Alphonsus intuitively grasped that devotion to the heart of Jesus is devotion to the love of Jesus, the same love that had liberated him. And as he surveyed a society in which secularism was on the rise, Christians were boomeranging between legalism and laxity, and even the devout were flitting from one spiritual fad to another seeking quick fixes for their faults, Alphonsus recognized the need for greater devotion to the heart of Jesus. As he explains in his 1758 booklet on the Sacred Heart:

> *So many persons . . . pay much attention to the practice of various devotions but neglect this; and . . . many preachers and confessors . . . say a great many things, but speak little of love for Jesus Christ: whereas love for Jesus Christ, ought to be the principal, indeed the only, devotion of a Christian. . . . This neglect is the reason why souls make so little progress in virtue.*

In his usual erudite-yet-direct fashion, Alphonsus made a compelling case for the devotion and reminded its critics that when we honor Christ's heart, we honor all of Him. To depict the pierced human heart of Jesus craving our love isn't to denigrate His divinity but to affirm the biblical truth that our infinite Creator humbles Himself to draw near to finite creatures. "Jesus has no need of us; He is equally happy . . . with or without our love," Alphonsus writes, yet "He desires our love . . . as if His happiness depended on that of man." That longing for love is simply a consequence of who God is: "He Who loves necessarily desires to be loved. The heart requires the heart; love seeks love . . ."

Alphonsus and his writings played a decisive role in popularizing devotion to the Sacred Heart, and the Sacred Heart feast day he lobbied for won a spot on the Church's liturgical calendar less than a decade after his book was published. As devotion to the heart of Jesus surged among the faithful, Jansenist ideas began to lose ground.

Yet even after the official collapse of Jansenism in the early eighteenth century, its image of a vengeful, fearsome God haunted the Church through the nineteenth century. That's when Thérèse of Lisieux, perhaps the most popular recovering perfectionist saint of all time, took love for the heart of Jesus to a new level.

If there's a darling of the Communion of Saints, an endearingly impish baby sister whose candor and antics make even the infamously cranky Saint Jerome laugh, surely it's Saint Thérèse.

The youngest of nine children born to French parents who have themselves been canonized, Thérèse arrived frail and fragile in 1873. Her mother, Saint Zélie Martin, had lost four older children in infancy or early childhood, and doctors said Thérèse might soon follow. But Thérèse had strength the doctors couldn't see, and soon Zélie was describing her as "a big baby, tanned by the sun" who "smiles continuously" and is "very sweet and very advanced for her age."

Unfortunately, Thérèse and her mother weren't able to enjoy each other for long. Zélie died of breast cancer when Thérèse was only four, leaving her to be raised—and coddled—by her father, Louis, and her four older sisters. This "little queen" of the Martin family was sweet but stubborn, prone to what Zélie had labeled "frightful tantrums." After her mother's death, Thérèse was also prone to scruples, sadness, and hypersensitivity.

A Christmas night conversion on the cusp of her fourteenth birthday—when Thérèse overheard her father lamenting her childishness and managed not to collapse into her usual tears—ushered her into new spiritual maturity. Within the year, Thérèse was lobbying everyone from the local bishop to the pope for permission to enter the Carmelite convent where two of her older sisters were already nuns. The normal entry age was twenty-one; Thérèse entered at fifteen.

Her willfulness, hypersensitivity, and hunger for approval followed her there. Surrounded by what biographer Joseph Schmidt calls "critical mothers" and rattled by the fire-and-brimstone homilies of Jansenist-influenced priests, Thérèse was brought face-to-face with the same feelings of abandonment, rejection, grief, and victimhood that had plunged her into an intense psychosomatic illness at age ten. She found herself nursing impatience and anger toward the women she had chosen to spend her life with and wondering how God would answer her desires for holiness when she was clearly too weak to meet the impossible standards of perfection set before her.

Gradually, over the course of the nine years Thérèse spent in the convent before her death from tuberculosis at age twenty-four, she came to realize that the very striving after flawlessness she had once seen as essential to holiness was actually getting in the way of what God wanted to do in her soul. So little by little, through prayer, life experience, and a close reading of Scripture, Thérèse began to formulate a new spirituality.

Her "little way of confidence and love," as it became known, is grounded in a truth Thérèse discovered in Paul's First Letter to the Corinthians. There Paul lists the many parts and gifts of the Body of Christ before describing what he calls the "still more excellent way" and "the greatest" spiritual gift: love (1 Cor. 12:31, 13:13). When she read that passage, Thérèse heard the Lord speaking straight to her.

All her life, Thérèse had been a person of great aspirations, an overachiever for whom the status quo or one narrow option was never enough. When presented with a choice of dresses for her dolls at age two, Thérèse waited until her older sister had selected one, then she grabbed the whole basket, declaring as she marched off: "I choose all!" That bottomless hunger for more—for something bigger, something deeper, and, yes, something perfect—had never left her. "I feel within me other vocations," Thérèse wrote once, ". . . the vocation of the warrior, the priest, the apostle, the doctor, the martyr."

In Paul's words, Thérèse found the something more she was seeking. She found a way to be a saint in spite of her weakness: "O Jesus, my love . . . my vocation, at last I have found it. My vocation is love! . . . [I]n the heart of the Church, my Mother, I shall be *Love*. Thus I shall be everything . . ."

To be love in the heart of the Church, for Thérèse, meant that she no longer had to deny her faults, her failures, or her ugly feelings. She only had to face her wounds honestly and offer them back to Jesus each time they came to her attention, trusting that if she cooperated with His grace and kept trying to love as He loves, He would take care of the rest. She could let go of getting better, getting credit, and getting even, let go of protecting herself or detecting how far she had advanced on what she called "the rough stairway of fear."

Thérèse had discovered a faster way, "the elevator of love." And it led straight to the heart of Christ.

From at least the age of twelve, when Thérèse enrolled herself in the Jesuit-run Apostleship of Prayer—an international network of Christians who pray daily to unite themselves with the Sacred Heart—she harbored special affection for Christ's heart. That affection ripened into passionate love once Thérèse discovered her little way.

Thérèse saw the heart of Jesus as the answer to her infinite, insatiable longing for love, a longing no human being had ever managed to satisfy. As she wrote in a poem about the Sacred Heart composed two years before her death,

> I need a heart burning with tenderness
> Who will be my support forever,
> Who loves everything in me, even my weakness . . .
> And who never leaves me day or night.

Calling Christ's heart her "only hope," Thérèse asks to "hide myself in Your Sacred Heart," wounds and sins and all. Despite her faults, Thérèse says, "I do not fear, my virtue is You!"

To refuse to fear was a bold move in Thérèse's day. The long shadow of Jansenism had distorted even the Sacred Heart devotion for many Catholics by that point, shifting their focus from God's merciful love to their own unworthiness of love and need to atone for sin.

Thérèse considered the Sacred Heart an invitation to intimacy, not another goad to guilt. "I myself do not see the Sacred Heart as everybody else," she says. "I think that the Heart of my Spouse is mine alone, just as mine is His alone, and I speak to Him then in the solitude of this delightful heart to heart, while waiting to contemplate Him one day face to face."

Her confidence didn't spring from pride or complacency. Thérèse recognized her unworthiness and practiced plenty of self-denial. She resisted even small sins vigorously, refusing to retaliate when other nuns berated her, accused her unfairly, or sat at the end of her sickbed as she lay dying and laughed at her, as one was wont to do. She gave her best smiles to the crabbiest sisters, spent years shivering silently in a frigid bedroom, and suffered a torturous eighteen-month dark night of the soul during which she felt no hint of God's love, even as she kept on loving Him. No sacrifice for Jesus was too big or too small: Thérèse even practiced love amid the laundry, working without complaint next to a coworker who splashed dirty water on her with every dunk and rinse. As she explained once to another nun,

> Don't think that to follow the path of love means to follow the path of repose, full of sweetness and consolations. It is completely the opposite. To offer oneself as a victim to Love means to give oneself up without any reservations to whatever God pleases, which means to expect to share with Jesus His humiliations, His chalice of bitterness.

Thérèse was willing to drink deeply from that chalice, but she didn't think God was asking her to punish herself with severe penances, obsessive guilt, or compulsive tracking of her virtues and vices. Nor had it escaped her notice that the same sisters who had treated her harshly as a young nun were consumed with loathing for themselves and their faults.

As Schmidt explains in his masterful guides to her spirituality, *Walking the Little Way of Thérèse of Lisieux* and *Everything Is Grace*, Thérèse discerned a latent streak of violence in the perfectionist spirituality of her day and in herself, and she renounced it. Instead of striking back at those who hurt her, raging against her own flaws, or pouting over her misfortunes, Thérèse chose to continually bring her pain back to Jesus for healing and keep her broken heart open to His love, even when she wanted to shut down. She paid attention to her thoughts and feelings, not only her words and actions, because she knew that unforgiveness and self-pity are easier to uproot in the seedling stage than after they've sprouted into bitter, full-grown fruits. Thérèse didn't beat herself up over feelings she couldn't control, but she learned to pray through her emotions before acting on them to discover where fear, selfishness, or vindictiveness might be leading her off the path of love.

When Thérèse was made novice mistress of her convent, she shared this holistic, heart-centered approach with other young nuns. If they berated themselves for faults, she urged them to bear patiently with themselves and cast their faults into the "devouring fire of [God's] love." She gave her older sister Léonie, the problem child of the Martin family, the same advice: "God is much better than you believe. He is content with a glance, a sigh of love. . . . As for me, I find perfection very easy to practice because I have understood it is a matter of taking hold of Jesus by His Heart."

Not even the formidable standard that Jesus lays out in Matthew's Gospel—to "love your enemies" and "be perfect as your heavenly Father is perfect"—could shake Thérèse's confidence. She knew she couldn't meet that standard on her own. She also knew she didn't have to. She needed only to unite her heart with Christ's and let His love shine through her weakness.

"When I am charitable," Thérèse says, "it is Jesus alone who is acting in me."

As for loving God with her whole heart, that, too, was a task Thérèse entrusted to the heart of Christ: "To love You as You love me, I must borrow Your love."

Loving and forgiving herself was perhaps the greatest challenge for perfectionist Thérèse. It took years, but Thérèse eventually came to see that the call to love our enemies extends even to what Schmidt dubs "the enemy within"—our own weakness and wounds. As biographer Bishop Patrick Ahern notes, "she saw clearly that, in approaching God, weakness is not a *liability*. It is in fact an *asset*."

Two years before her death, Thérèse wrote an "Act of Oblation to Merciful Love." In it, the woman who would be named the youngest Doctor of the Church in history and hailed as the "greatest saint of modern times" by Pope Pius X tells Jesus of the new desires that have replaced her earlier cravings for approval, appreciation, and security:

> . . . *I do not want to lay up merits for heaven. I want to work for Your Love alone with the one purpose of pleasing You, consoling Your Sacred Heart, and saving souls who will love You eternally.*

> *In the evening of this life, I shall appear before You with empty hands, for I do not ask You, Lord, to count my works. All our justice is stained in Your eyes. I wish, then, to be clothed in Your own Justice and to receive from Your Love the eternal possession of Yourself. I want no other Throne, no other Crown but You, my Beloved!*

I love Thérèse. I really do.

Ask me my favorite saint and I'll hem and haw a bit, but at the end of the day, I always come back to Thérèse. I love her passion, her humor, her spunk. I love how frankly she admits faults that most of us spend a lifetime trying to hide.

After Teresa of Ávila, Thérèse was the first saint I befriended as an adult. Her writings about her father's battle with dementia helped me get through my own father's battle with Alzheimer's. I named my first daughter, Maryrose Therese, for her.

I love Thérèse. And when my mother gave me Schmidt's books a few years ago, and I learned more about her struggle with perfectionism, I loved her even more.

And yet . . .

Grinning and bearing it while someone snickers at you on your deathbed? Saddling up to the arch-grouch of the convent and offering to feed her, walk her to the bathroom, and spend your few precious moments of free time each day sewing beside her as she tells you nonstop that you're doing it wrong? Telling Jesus that after all those sacrifices in this life, He can hold the rewards of the next because you're only in it for love?

Really?

The open-heart spirituality of Thérèse is admirable and lovely, a sure antidote to perfectionism. But I struggle to imagine imitating her. Sometimes I wonder if I even want to.

For that matter, do I want to imitate Francis of Assisi as he courts the same public rejection and ridicule that Jesus endured on the cross? Or join Jane de Chantal in forgiving relatives who bully me, cheat me, and mistreat my children? Or spend my last years as Alphonsus Liguori did, refusing to retaliate as I watch former friends steal my life's work and expel me from a community I founded?

Thérèse says the path of love isn't all sweetness and consolations. I'd say that's putting it mildly. Looking at the sacrifices it entailed for her and her fellow saints, I'm tempted to think the prison of perfectionism isn't such a bad option after all. At least I can control things there. I can decorate my cell, cozy it up with pious touches, maybe even accomplish a few good deeds. And I can continue to protect myself, to put plenty of righteous indignation and rationalization and a long record of wrongs between me and anyone who hurts me. I can avoid vulnerability so as to avoid, or at least minimize, pain.

The trouble with that approach, of course, is that pain is inevitable. I'm going to suffer in this life either way. The question is whether I'll find meaning and value in that suffering, whether I'll allow God to use my pain for His purposes—or not.

In theory, I'm willing to let God work through my wounds, to let Him turn them into conduits of mercy for others, even those who've hurt me.

In reality, in the nitty-gritty reality of my life, today—that's another story. That means I have to repent of at least half a dozen things I've thought or said since breakfast. And I have to abandon my attachments to security and control.

Those attachments run deep. They stretch back to my days as a quiet, sensitive, hyper-responsible little girl. I felt very vulnerable in a loud, often scary world where mean kids thrived and adults didn't always act like adults. I didn't like feeling vulnerable. So I controlled what I could—my grades, my looks, the anger and sadness I knew nice girls don't feel—and I even managed to make it look effortless.

Deep inside, though, I knew my control was tenuous. I could sense it on those nights when I'd wake up in a cold sweat, my heart racing from that recurring nightmare that always found me barreling down the highway at seventy miles an hour in the family station wagon. My parents and brother were in the backseat, too busy squawking about their own concerns to watch the road. I was watching it, though. I had to: I was the driver. And no matter how many compliments my passengers paid me on my steering skills, I couldn't shake the feeling that a crash was inevitable.

Because I was five. And my feet couldn't touch the pedals. And no one had taught me how to drive.

When I see the path of love walked by the saints, sometimes I feel the same panic I felt behind the wheel of that runaway car. It seems crazy to live like them, crazy to open my heart so wide to God's love that any lunatic could come trample on it.

And in a sense, it *is* crazy. If you look at it through the lens of cost-benefit analysis, if your goal is to come out a winner in the world's eyes, it isn't worth the risk.

There are rewards, though. And as I've discovered since I started trying to walk this path—emphasis on the *trying*—they're not all reserved to the next life.

The most obvious reward is that I see myself and my perfectionist predicament more clearly. Since I started looking at the movements of my heart in the light of faith, asking if the way I'm feeling or thinking about a person or situation reflects the heart of Christ, I've uncovered many hidden pockets of resentment, judgment, and self-pity that need healing. Recognizing and repenting of them isn't particularly pleasant. I feel like I'm apologizing all over the place these days and I probably still don't apologize half as much as I should. Yet I understand my daily need for God's mercy, and the value of that mercy, as never before.

Living this way is also simpler. I spot my mistakes sooner and waste less energy rationalizing or running from them. I still worry too much about externals: *Do I seem angry or unforgiving? Will I look uncharitable if I do this?* But I have less time to worry about how I look to others now that I'm worrying more about how I look to God.

I don't know how much my outward behavior yet reflects the changes in my heart, but I hope I'm moving toward a greater share of that split-second freedom that a spiritual director once described to me. She said when we first set out trying to overcome deep-seated sinful tendencies, we can hardly tell which end is up and it takes a two-by-four to get our attention. If we respond to God's gift of grace and repent of the sins we see, the Holy Spirit blesses our cooperation by giving us more grace to see more sins and to see them sooner after we commit them. It can feel as if things are getting worse rather than better. But if we hang in there and respond to *that* grace—by repenting early and often—we receive still more grace, which helps us spot sins before we commit them. Sometimes it's only a split second before, a mere heartbeat to reconsider. It's a new measure of freedom, though, and it's ours for the asking.

It's the same with forgiveness. Its reward is greater freedom, but first you have to pass through risk, uncertainty, and discomfort. It's a little like reaching for help when you're drowning. It feels safer to cling to the drowning swimmer next to you, even though doing so is only dragging you down faster, than to let go and grab the life preserver. But it's only when we pry our fingers off our grudges and those who caused them that we can grasp the freedom God wills for us. If I want to be fully healed, I must fully forgive—"seventy times seven" and "from the heart," as Jesus commands (Matt. 18:22, 35).

That's tough, as tough as it gets. As I told a priest in Confession recently, "I *try* to forgive. I *think* I've forgiven. But then they do the same things all over again and when they do, I realize I'm still angry about what they did before. It's never-ending."

His answer: "Pray for a forgiving heart."

It's the best advice I've heard. Because when it comes to pardoning someone for decades-old patterns of sin that they show no sign of acknowledging, much less changing, forgiveness is not a matter of mere will or skill. It's a grace.

While we pray for that grace, it helps to recognize that forgiveness is not the same as reconciliation. We can forgive unilaterally but reconciliation requires the other person's change of heart, too. Some relationships won't be restored this side of heaven, even after we forgive.

Which leads to perhaps the most unexpected reward that comes with trying to love as Christ loves: discovering that it doesn't mean becoming a doormat.

To love someone is to want what's best for that person. Codependency isn't love; enabling bad behavior isn't love; pretending you don't mind abuse or sin isn't love. A prayerful person may choose to endure mistreatment for love of God if that's what God has called her to do. But much of what gets passed off as Christian charity is perfectionist people-pleasing in disguise. It's not about leading others to Christ; it's about making ourselves look better or avoiding conflict or winning approval. It's about fear, not love.

The more I remember to pray before reacting to unsettling people or situations, the more I've noticed Jesus nudging me away from fear—even when that means saying no to what seems like the nice Christian thing to do. God never sanctions sin; He doesn't give me a license to respond rudely to demands I don't want to meet. What He does give me is peace, along with frequent reminders in prayer that it can be loving to set limits, to conserve my time, to prioritize the needs of my children and husband and even my own need to care for myself. It can be loving to say no. And I can say no without rancor or guilt, confident that my answer is coming from love, because it came to me from Him.

British politician Andrew Bennett once said, "The longest journey you will ever take is the 18 inches from your head to your heart."

My journey from head knowledge of perfectionism to heart change began with a bleeding toddler in an emergency-room parking lot. It has continued as I've researched the lives of perfectionist saints in recent years, testing their advice in the rough-and-tumble of daily life. But my head-to-heart journey didn't kick into high gear until Thanksgiving weekend 2017, when my seventy-seven-year-old mother fell down a flight of stairs and suffered a traumatic brain injury.

She was on a blood thinner at the time, an irreversible one, and the bleeding in her brain was severe. I spent three days by her side in the ICU, watching her grow progressively more disoriented. I was praying she wouldn't need surgery because the neurosurgeon said she probably wouldn't survive it, at least until the blood thinner cleared her system.

On the third day after her accident, when I was perched alone at her bedside and punchy from lack of sleep, the neurosurgeon stormed in and told me he couldn't wait any longer. Her condition was tanking and the pressure of all that blood in her brain was threatening to cause herniation—a condition in which the swollen brain runs out of room and can wind up pushing through a hole in the base of the skull. The usual result is death.

"She's in a life-threatening situation," he barked. "I think we need to do a lobectomy."

My head lurched back as if I'd been struck. I felt tears rolling down my cheeks as I pictured a glassy-eyed Jack Nicholson in the last reels of *One Flew Over the Cuckoo's Nest.*

"Is that like a lobotomy?"

"It's a *lobectomy*. I want to remove her frontal lobe. To make space for the swelling. I need your answer in fifteen minutes."

The surgeon swept past me and out of the room. My hands began to shake as I fumbled for my phone to call John. He was driving the kids home from violin practice and could barely make out what I was saying over their squeals and my sobs.

"I'll be over as quick as I can," he said, but I wasn't sure it would be quick enough.

I called my brother, who had come in from Kansas City the night of Mom's accident but had since returned home. He wasn't picking up.

I looked at my mother, laying there semi-comatose. *Would she even want to live without her frontal lobe? Would anyone?* I pictured Dad in his final years, his brain so decimated by dementia that he couldn't remember my name or where he was or even how to swallow.

"I don't want to do this again," I told Mom's nurse, who began planting tissues in my trembling hands. "My dad died of Alzheimer's. I can't do this again. Not this. Not brain stuff."

I sent a garbled text begging for prayers to my friend Judy in Philadelphia, who wrote back to tell me she was on it. Then I did the only thing I could think of: I ran to the hospital chapel.

"Help," I whispered, as I crumpled onto the ground in front of the tabernacle where the Eucharist is reposed. "Jesus, I can't do this without You. I can't do this. Please help me. *Please.*"

I felt so vulnerable in that moment, so little and weak. All those old feelings from childhood—of abandonment, of carrying the world on my shoulders, of being trapped in a terrifying situation that I didn't create and couldn't fix—came flooding back. It was just like that night outside the ER.

Except this time something was different. I felt the same fear and inadequacy but now I also felt something else, something I can only describe as sweetness. I felt very near to Jesus and He felt very near to me. Sitting with my feet tucked under my knees, wet tissues clutched to my pounding heart, I could almost feel His heart keeping time with mine. I took a deep breath, savoring this flash of warmth in the midst of what felt like the coldest day of my life. When I exhaled, I knew Jesus was with me, that I didn't have to do this alone.

I walked out of the chapel a few minutes later. I still didn't know what to do. But I knew that I could live with whatever choice I made, because I was doing my best. That was enough for God. And to my surprise, it was enough for me, too.

Within an hour, a seemingly impossible choice became clearer. John made it to the hospital in time to talk to the surgeon, who came up with another option when he saw how distraught I was about the lobectomy. He offered to do a craniectomy, a removal of part of Mom's skull flap which would allow her brain to swell safely while keeping her frontal lobe intact. After the swelling receded, he said, we could do another surgery to put the flap back on. We tracked down my brother and put him on speakerphone for the conversation, and the three of us decided it was our best bet.

Six months, three brain surgeries, a dozen moves between medical facilities, and several more infections, falls, and crises later, Mom is still with us. She's in a wheelchair now, due to brain damage sustained from the heavy bleeding immediately after her fall. I'm not sure she'll ever walk or live independently again. But she's still with us, she's still feisty and funny and fully aware, and she still has her brain—all of it.

In the pressure cooker of the past six months, as I've found myself managing every aspect of my mother's life and care with only John to help me, all of my perfectionist temptations have flared up: my tendencies toward hurry and harshness, my unrealistic expectations and false guilt, my penchant for neglecting self-care and indulging in self-pity. The hectic task of balancing family and work has become herculean. Burnout is a constant threat. So is resentment and unforgiveness toward those who I thought would step up to help but haven't.

What's kept me going are the lessons I've learned from my kindred spirits in heaven, the recovering perfectionist saints. I can't imagine trying to navigate the ups and downs of the past six months without their wisdom, while still operating under my old perfectionist illusions. That first excruciating medical decision probably would have done me in, and if not that, then one of the dozens that followed.

Not that I'm acing my crash-course in overcoming perfectionism. This former A-plus student is happy to pull down a solid C most weeks. Challenging as it is to pursue Gospel perfection these days—to be gentle with myself and others, to slow down and breathe when everything around me is falling apart, to remember that it's God's job to judge and not mine—it's also a joy. While the pursuit of worldly perfection is miserable and grueling even when you seem close to pulling it off, the path of love is littered with rewards along the way. Even when I find myself still tripping over my own feet a few steps from the starting line, I'm glad I'm on it. It's the path that leads to life, the abundant life that Jesus promises (John 10:10). And that's where I want to head.

There's another perk of walking this path, the reason I sought it out in the first place: My children are learning alongside me. Unlike my quest for the phantom of worldly perfection, the pursuit of Christian perfection doesn't require me to have it all figured out before I can teach them. Just as the saints taught me through their failures as well as their successes, so I'm teaching my kids through those mistakes that I make and then admit right before their eyes. When I follow a rant they overheard with a prayer for the person I was angry with or a too-sharp rebuke with a swift apology, they learn something. They see that mistakes are inevitable, that forgiveness is possible, that they can treat themselves with compassion because that's not just what Mommy says, it's what Mommy does.

Last week, as the Feast of the Sacred Heart was approaching, I asked the kids at lunch what they knew about it. Had they ever looked at that picture in our front hall? Why is Jesus pointing to His heart? And why are there flames coming out of it?

"Because His heart is burning with love for us!" eight-year-old Maryrose answered, beaming and half-bouncing out of her chair the way she does when she's really excited.

"But what if we make big mistakes?" I asked. "Does He love us a little less?"

"No!" Maryrose shouted, now standing and shaking her grilled cheese sandwich for emphasis, her smile as wide as the sun. "He loves us *no matter what*."

She might never have learned that so well—I might never have learned that—were it not for that wound that sent me rushing to the emergency room years ago, and all the wounds and weaknesses I've uncovered in myself since.

It has healed now, my child's wound. It's a thin white scar that no one really notices except me. For years I prayed it would go away altogether, so I wouldn't have to remember my failure and heartache that day. I wondered why God wouldn't answer my prayer.

Now I think I know. He wanted me to see it and remember the healing truth it revealed: that I'm not perfect, and I don't have to be. And that He loves me anyway—always and forever, and perfectly.

RECOMMENDED FURTHER READING

These are some books by and about recovering perfectionist saints that I found helpful:

JANE DE CHANTAL AND FRANCIS DE SALES

Francis de Sales, Jane de Chantal: Letters of Spiritual Direction, Classics of Western Spirituality series, translated by Peronne Marie Thibert, V.H.M., selected and introduced by Wendy M. Wright and Joseph F. Power, O.S.F.S. (New York: Paulist Press, 1988).

Introduction to the Devout Life, Francis de Sales, translated by John K. Ryan (New York: Image, 2003).

Heart Speaks to Heart: The Salesian Tradition, Wendy M. Wright, Traditions of Christian Spirituality series, edited by Philip Sheldrake (Maryknoll, New York: Orbis Books, 2004).

The Life of Saint Jane Frances Fremyot de Chantal, Emily Bowles, Quarterly Series: Second Volume (London: Burns and Oates, 1872).

Madame de Chantal: Portrait of a Saint, Elisabeth Stopp (Westminster, MD: The Newman Press, 1963).

St. Jane Frances de Chantal, Janet Mary Scott (London/Glasgow: Sands & Co. Ltd., 1948).

Saint Jeanne de Chantal, Andre Ravier, S.J. (San Francisco: Ignatius Press, 1989).

Francis de Sales: Sage & Saint, Andre Ravier, S.J., trans. by Joseph D. Bowler, O.S.F.S. (San Francisco: Ignatius Press, 1988).

ALPHONSUS LIGUORI

The Practice of the Love of Jesus Christ, Alphonsus Liguori, translated by Peter Heinegg with an introduction by J. Robert Fenili, C.Ss.R. (Liguori, MO: Liguori Publications, 1997).

Alphonsus de Liguori: Selected Writings, Classics of Western Spirituality series, edited by Frederick M. Jones, C.Ss.R., with the collaboration of Brendan McConvery, C.Ss.R., Raphael Gallagher, C.Ss.R., Terrence J. Moran, C.Ss.R., and Martin McKeever, C.Ss.R. (New York: Paulist Press, 1999).

Alphonsus Liguori: The Redeeming Love of Christ, A Collection of Spiritual Writings, edited by Joseph Oppitz, C.Ss.R. (New York: New City Press, 1992).

St. Alphonsus Liguori: Tireless Worker for the Most Abandoned, Theodule Rey-Mermet, C.Ss.R., translated from the Second French Edition (1987) by Jehanne-Marie Marchesi, English edition prepared by the staff of Liguori Publications (Brooklyn, NY: New City Press, 1989).

Alphonsus de Liguori: The Saint of Bourbon Naples, 1696–1787, Frederick M. Jones, C.Ss.R. (Westminster, MD: Christian Classics, Inc., 1992).

IGNATIUS OF LOYOLA

The Spiritual Exercises of Saint Ignatius: A New Translation Based on Studies in the Language of the Autograph, translated by Louis J. Puhl, S.J. (Chicago: Loyola University Press, 1951).

The Discernment of Spirits: An Ignatian Guide for Everyday Living, Timothy M. Gallagher, O.M.V. (New York: Crossroad, 2005).

The Examen Prayer: Ignatian Wisdom for Our Lives Today, Timothy M. Gallagher, O.M.V. (New York: Crossroad, 2006).

Spiritual Consolation: An Ignatian Guide for Greater Discernment of Spirits, Timothy M. Gallagher, O.M.V. (New York: Crossroad, 2007).

Discerning the Will of God: An Ignatian Guide to Christian Decision Making, Timothy M. Gallagher, O.M.V. (New York: Crossroad, 2009).

Draw Me into Your Friendship: A Literal Translation and a Contemporary Reading of the Spiritual Exercises, David L. Fleming, S.J. (St. Louis: Institute of Jesuit Sources, 1996).

Ignatius of Loyola: The Psychology of a Saint, W. W. Meissner, S.J., M.D. (New Haven and London: Yale University Press, 1992).

BENEDICT OF NURSIA

The Rule of St. Benedict, translated, with introduction and notes by Anthony C. Meisel and M. L. del Mastro (New York: Image, 1975).

The Cloister Walk, Kathleen Norris (New York: Riverhead Books, 1996).

Living with Contradiction: Reflections on the Rule of St. Benedict, Esther de Waal (San Francisco: Harper & Row, 1989).

Seeking God: The Way of St. Benedict, Esther de Waal (Collegeville, MN: The Liturgical Press, 1984, 2001).

St. Benedict, Blessed by God, Guy-Marie Oury, O.S.B., translated by Rev. John A. Otto (Collegeville, MN: The Liturgical Press, 1980).

St. Benedict: A Character Study, Rt. Rev. Ildephonsus Herwegen, O.S.B., translated by Dom Peter Nugent, O.S.B. (London: Sands & Co., 1924).

FRANCIS OF ASSISI

Francis and Clare: The Complete Works, Classics of Western Spirituality series, translation and introduction by Regis J. Armstrong, O.F.M. Cap., and Ignatius C. Brady, O.F.M. (New York: Paulist Press, 1982).

Francis: A Biography of the Saint of Assisi, Michael de la Bédoyère (New York: Harper & Row, 1962).

Saint Francis of Assisi, Msgr. Leon Cristiani, translated by M. Angeline Bouchard (Boston: St. Paul Editions/Daughters of St. Paul, 1975).

Following Francis of Assisi: A Spirituality for Daily Living, Patti Normile (Cincinnati: St. Anthony Messenger Press, 1996).

The Richest of Poor Men: The Spirituality of St. Francis of Assisi, John R. H. Moorman (Huntington, IN: Our Sunday Visitor, 1977).

THÉRÈSE OF LISIEUX

Story of a Soul: The Autobiography of Saint Thérèse of Lisieux, A Study Edition, translated by John Clarke, O.C.D., prepared by Marc Foley, O.C.D. (Washington, DC: ICS Publications, 2005, 2016).

Everything Is Grace: The Life and Way of Thérèse of Lisieux, Joseph F. Schmidt, F.S.C. (Ijamsville, MD: The Word Among Us Press, 2007).

Walking the Little Way of Thérèse of Lisieux: Discovering the Path of Love, Joseph F. Schmidt, F.S.C. (Frederick, MD: The Word Among Us Press, 2012).

Maurice and Thérèse: The Story of a Love, Patrick Ahern (New York: Image, 2001).

A Family of Saints: The Martins of Lisieux, Saints Thérèse, Louis, and Zelie, Fr. Stephane-Joseph Piat, O.F.M., translated by a Benedictine of Stanbrook Abbey (San Francisco: Ignatius Press, 2016).

MORE ON THE SACRED HEART OF JESUS

Heart of the Redeemer: An Apologia for the Contemporary and Perennial Value of the Devotion to the Sacred Heart of Jesus, Timothy T. O'Donnell (San Francisco: Ignatius Press, 1992).

A Heart on Fire: Rediscovering Devotion to the Sacred Heart of Jesus, James Kubicki, S.J. (Notre Dame, IN: Ave Maria Press, 2012).

ACKNOWLEDGMENTS

"Gratitude," G. K. Chesterton once said, "is happiness doubled by wonder."

I've been blessed by more than my share of happy, wonder-filled moments these past nine years, as my husband and I have plunged into the long-awaited adventure of parenthood that sparked and shaped this book. And so it is to my four children—Maryrose Therese, John Patrick, Clara Colleen, and Joseph Francis—that I dedicate it.

Little friends, being your mother, and teacher, has been the privilege of a lifetime, a duty of delight that has taught me far more than I could ever teach you. It's difficult to put my love for you into words. If nothing else, I hope I've taught you this: that each of you is loved "with an everlasting love" (Jer. 31:3) by God as well as your father and me. And nothing you do or don't do could ever separate you from that love (Rom. 8: 38–39).

Of course, my little ones wouldn't exist—and I wouldn't have time to write books while homeschooling them—were it not for the love and support of my husband, John Allan Campbell. John was my sounding board, first reader, and chief encourager for this book, as he is for all I do. John believed in this book and in me even when I didn't. He put that belief into action day after day, by taking the kids on Saturdays and evenings so I could write, helping with homeschooling on Wednesday and Thursday mornings so I could write some more, and staying up late countless nights to talk through my ideas and frustrations so I could keep writing. He also stepped up in an extraordinary way to oversee the medical care my mother received in the wake of her traumatic brain injury this past year, and his selfless dedication saved her life more than once. John is my rock, my partner, the love of my life. And I am blessed to be his wife. I love you, John. Forever.

I am grateful to my parents, Thomas Patrick and Mary Beatrice Carroll, for sharing the gift of faith with me, and for witnessing to God's steadfast love throughout their thirty-eight-year marriage and my father's twelve-year battle with Alzheimer's disease. The first book that hooked me on the saints was a gift from my dad; most of the rest were gifts from my mom. I thank God for their love and prayers, and for the continued gift of my mother's life. I'm glad you're still with us, Mom.

I appreciate my agent, Lisa Jackson, who helped me find the right home for this book and offered valuable support through the publishing process; my editor, Beth Adams, who enthusiastically embraced this book and worked diligently with the Howard/Atria team to ensure its success; Kelly Hughes, who led the charge on publicity; and Bill Barry, whose comments on an early draft helped me refine my focus.

I am thankful for my dear friend Judy Wilson, who has been a source of encouragement, prayers, and help for years but in a particular way during my mom's recent health crisis.

Last on this list, but first in my heart, is Jesus. He loved me into being, has loved me through all the twists and turns of my journey, and continues to love me despite my daily stumbles and grumbles, my dry spells and faltering trust. It is Jesus who inspired this book, Jesus who made it possible. And whatever good this book does belongs completely and totally to Jesus, as do I.

Colleen Carroll Campbell
Feast of Christ the King
November 25, 2018